JAMESTOWN EDUCATION

D1242476

SIGNATURE READING

LEVEL D

McGraw Hill Glencoe

New York, New York   Columbus, Ohio   Chicago, Illinois   Peoria, Illinois   Woodland Hills, California

Reviewers

Marsha Miller, Ed.D
Reading Specialist
Elgin High School
1200 Maroon Drive
Elgin, IL 60120

Kati Pearson
Orange County Public Schools
Literacy Coordinator
Carver Middle School
4500 West Columbia Street
Orlando, FL 32811

Lynda Pearson
Assistant Principal
Reading Specialist
Lied Middle School
5350 Tropical Parkway
Las Vegas, NV 89130

Suzanne Zweig
Reading Specialist/Consultant
Sullivan High School
6631 N. Bosworth
Chicago, IL 60626

Cover Image: Donald E. Carroll/Getty Images

 **Glencoe**

The *McGraw-Hill* Companies

ISBN: 0-07-861716-2 (Pupil's Edition)
ISBN: 0-07-861717-0 (Annotated Teacher's Edition)

Send all queries to:
Glencoe/McGraw-Hill
8787 Orion Place
Columbus, OH 43240-4027

8 9 113 09 08

Contents

How to Use This Book

Working Through the Lessons

The following descriptions will help you work your way through the lessons in this book.

Building Background will help you get ready to read. In this section you might begin a chart, discuss a question, or learn more about the topic of the selection.

Vocabulary Builder will help you start thinking about—and using—the selection vocabulary. You might draw a diagram and label it with vocabulary words, make a word map, match vocabulary words to their synonyms or antonyms, or use the words to predict what might happen in the selection.

Strategy Builder will introduce you to the strategy that you will use to read the selection. First you will read a definition of the strategy. Then you will see an example of how to use it. Often, you will be given ways to better organize or visualize what you will be reading.

Strategy Break will appear within the reading selection. It will show you how to apply the strategy you just learned to the first part of the selection.

Strategy Follow-up will ask you to apply the same strategy to the second part of the selection. Most of the time, you will work on your own to complete this section. Sometimes, however, you might work with a partner or a group of classmates.

Personal Checklist questions will ask you to rate how well you did in the lesson. When you finish totaling your score, you will enter it on the graphs on page 203.

Vocabulary Check will follow up on the work you did in the Vocabulary Builder. After you total your score, you will enter it on page 203.

Strategy Check will follow up on the strategy work that you did in the lesson. After you total your score, you will enter it on page 203.

Comprehension Check will check your understanding of the selection. After you total your score, you will enter it on page 203.

Extending will give ideas for activities that are related to the selection. Some activities will help you learn more about the topic of the selection. Others might ask you to respond to the selection by dramatizing, writing, or drawing something.

Resources such as books, recordings, videos, and Web sites will help you complete the Extending activities.

Graphing Your Progress

The information and graphs on pages 202–203 will help you track your progress as you work through this book. **Graph 1** will help you record your scores for the Personal Checklist and the Vocabulary, Strategy, and Comprehension Checks. **Graph 2** will help you track your overall progress across the book. You'll be able to see your areas of strength, as well as any areas that could use improvement. You and your teacher can discuss ways to work on those areas.

LESSON ❶ The Hole in the Road

village

silly

mayor

deep

hole

dangerous

soapsuds

rainwater

bridge

Building Background

What do you call a frog that's stuck in mud?
"Unhoppy."

What did one road say to the other road?
"Hi, Way!"

What did the dirt say during a rainstorm?
"If this keeps up, my name will be mud."

Did you smile or laugh as you read any of these jokes? The creators of the jokes had a purpose for writing them: to entertain you. What other things that you have read or seen lately were meant to be entertaining?

Authors write for one or more of these purposes: to **entertain** (make you laugh), to **inform** (explain or describe something), to **persuade** (try to get you to agree with their opinion), to **express** (share their feelings or ideas about something). For what purpose or purposes do you predict Helen Ketteman wrote "The Hole in the Road"?

Vocabulary Builder

1. Read the list of words in the margin. They are from the story "The Hole in the Road."

2. On the clipboards, write a meaning for each word. If a word has more than one meaning, predict how it might be used in the story and use that meaning.

3. Then use the vocabulary words and the title to help you predict what might happen in this story. Write your predictions on a separate sheet of paper. Use as many vocabulary words as possible.

4. Save your work. You will use it again in the Vocabulary Check.

CLIPBOARD

village

silly

mayor

deep

hole

CLIPBOARD

dangerous

soapsuds

rainwater

bridge

Strategy Builder

Identifying Problems and Solutions

- In some stories, the main character or characters have a **problem.** Throughout the story, the characters try to solve the problem. Sometimes they try more than one **solution.** By the end of the story, they usually come up with the solution that works—the **end result.**

- As you read the following paragraph, notice Lilly's problem and what she does to solve it. Do you think the end result is a good one? Why or why not?

> One day, Lilly got two party invitations in the mail. She was very excited until she noticed that both parties were on the same day. She didn't know what to do. She studied the invitations again. She discovered that the times of the parties were different. "I have an idea!" she said. "Kenny's party is from noon to 4:00, and Audrey's party is from 2:00 to 6:00. First I'll go to Kenny's party from noon to 2:45. Then I'll go to Audrey's party from 3:15 to 6:00. That way, I'll be able to go to both parties."

- If you wanted to show the problem and solutions in the paragraph above, you could create a **problem-solution frame.** It would look something like this:

What is the problem?
Lilly has been invited to two parties.

Why is it a problem?
Both parties are on the same day.

Solutions | **Results**

1. Lilly studied the invitations carefully. 1. She discovered that the times were different.

2. She divided up the times and decided to go to one party from noon to 2:45 and to the other party from 3:15 to 6:00. 2. **END RESULT:** Now she can go to both parties.

The Hole in the Road

by Helen Ketteman

As you read the first part of this story, notice the mayor's problem. (It is circled.) Then notice the solutions he tries, and the results of each one. (His solutions are underlined once. The results are underlined twice.) Why does the mayor keep trying new solutions?

Once there was an entire **village** of **silly** people. No one had a lick of sense, not even Mayor Moosebark or his assistant, Daniel Daniel.

Early one morning, the **mayor** strolled into town.

As he approached City Hall, he discovered a **deep hole** in the road. He leaned over the edge and peered in.

"This is awful!" he said. "People will fall in and hurt themselves. We must do something quickly!"

Mayor Moosebark ran to his assistant's house. Daniel Daniel's mother and father had named him Daniel Daniel in case they forgot one of his names.

Mayor Moosebark rang Daniel Daniel's doorbell. "Wake up!" the mayor shouted. "There is a **dangerous** hole in the road!"

The two men studied the hole, then sat by the edge to think. After a while, the mayor jumped up. "I know!" he shouted. "We will dig up the hole and carry it out of town!"

Daniel Daniel and Mayor Moosebark ran all over town, banging on every door. "Come to City Hall and bring your shovels!" they shouted. "There is important work to do!"

Soon all the townspeople were gathered at City Hall. "We must dig up this hole and carry it out of town," announced the mayor.

The people began working right away. But no matter how deep they dug, they could not reach the bottom of the hole.

Finally Mayor Moosebark stopped them. "This hole is too deep to dig up," he said. "We must try something else. We have made a mountain of dirt—perhaps we can fill the hole with that."

The people shoveled the dirt back into the hole. By the end of the day, the pile of dirt was gone, but the hole was still there, as big as ever.

"This is a very tricky hole," said the mayor. "Go home and rest. Tonight I will think of something else, and tomorrow we will try again."

 Stop here for the Strategy Break.

Strategy Break

If you were to create a problem-solution frame for the story so far, it might look like this:

> ### What is the problem?
> The mayor discovers a deep hole in the road near City Hall.
>
> ### Why is it a problem?
> The hole is dangerous. People could fall in and hurt themselves.

Solutions	Results
1. The townspeople try to dig up the hole and carry it out of town.	1. The hole gets deeper, and they can't reach the bottom.
2. They fill the hole with the dirt that they just dug out of it.	2. There is not enough dirt to fill the hole, so it's still there.

As you continue reading, keep paying attention to what the mayor does to try and solve the problem. Underline each solution once and each result twice. At the end of the story, you will create a problem-solution frame of your own.

 Go on reading to see what happens.

The next morning, Mayor Moosebark and Daniel Daniel rose early. "Today is washday in the village," said the mayor. "When the people wash clothes, they make lots of **soapsuds**. We will fill the hole with soapsuds."

Once again, the mayor and his assistant summoned the villagers. Everyone set to work scrubbing clothes. Soon there were huge piles of suds. The villagers filled their pails and dumped the suds into the hole. At last the hole was full. Everyone gathered around.

"Mayor Moosebark figured out how to fix this hole," said Daniel Daniel, "so he should have the honor of being the first to walk across it."

Mayor Moosebark puffed out his chest and stepped onto the soapsuds. At once, he disappeared. From somewhere under the suds he shouted, "Help! Get me out of here!"

Daniel Daniel got a rope and pulled the mayor out of the hole. The mayor went home to put on dry clothes. When he came back, the hole was almost empty.

"What happened to the soapsuds?" the mayor asked.

Daniel Daniel scratched his head. "I don't know where they went. They just went."

"It's just as well," said Mayor Moosebark. "They didn't work at all. I will think some more, and tomorrow we will try again."

As the mayor started home, a fat raindrop fell on this nose. "Water!" he shouted. "We will fill the hole with water!"

Daniel Daniel looked up at the black sky and said, "This time, the people won't have to work so hard. The rain will help."

It poured all night. The next morning, when Mayor Moosebark and Daniel Daniel checked the hole, **rainwater** had come all the way to the top. "It looks full," said the mayor.

"Any fool can see that," agreed Daniel Daniel. "Again, it should be your honor to walk across first."

The mayor stepped onto the water. He sank to the bottom, then floated to the top. "Help!" he shouted. "Get me out of here!"

Daniel Daniel got a rope and pulled the mayor out. "We did better this time," said Daniel Daniel. "At least you were on top of the water."

"We did better," agreed the mayor, "but not well enough. I have one more idea. I'm going home to change clothes. You round up the villagers."

When Mayor Moosebark returned, he said, "Our hole is now filled with water, but we must do one more thing. We must build a **bridge**. Then our hole will be fixed, and fixed right."

The people worked all day. By day's end, they had built a fine, strong bridge across the water-filled hole. The mayor stepped onto the bridge, and he didn't fall. He walked all the way across the hole. Everyone clapped and cheered. At last, their hole problem was solved.

If you happen upon that silly village today, you will find that the bridge is still there, strong as ever. But once in a while, the hole has to be filled with water. ●

Strategy Follow-up

Now create a problem-solution frame for the second part of "The Hole in the Road." For the Problem Box, use the information from the Strategy Break. Fill in the Solution Box with information from the second part of the story. Don't forget to label the end result.

What is the problem?
The mayor discovers a deep hole in the road near City Hall.

Why is it a problem?
The hole is dangerous. People could fall in and hurt themselves.

Solutions   **Results**

✓Personal Checklist

Read each question and put a check (✓) in the correct box.

1. In Building Background, how well were you able to predict Helen Ketteman's purpose for writing this story?
    - ☐ 3 (extremely well)
    - ☐ 2 (fairly well)
    - ☐ 1 (not well)

2. How well were you able to use the vocabulary words to predict what might happen in the story?
    - ☐ 3 (extremely well)
    - ☐ 2 (fairly well)
    - ☐ 1 (not well)

3. How well were you able to identify the solutions that the mayor tried in the second part of the story?
    - ☐ 3 (extremely well)
    - ☐ 2 (fairly well)
    - ☐ 1 (not well)

4. How well do you understand how the mayor finally solved the problem?
    - ☐ 3 (extremely well)
    - ☐ 2 (fairly well)
    - ☐ 1 (not well)

5. How well do you understand why the villagers have to add water to the hole every once in a while?
    - ☐ 3 (extremely well)
    - ☐ 2 (fairly well)
    - ☐ 1 (not well)

Vocabulary Check

Look back at the work you did in the Vocabulary Builder. Then answer each question by circling the correct letter.

1. Which sentence best describes the mayor's job in this story?
    - a. He runs the village.
    - b. He builds bridges.
    - c. He sells soapsuds.

2. Which vocabulary word best describes the people of the village?
    - a. dangerous
    - b. silly
    - c. deep

3. Which vocabulary word best describes the problem in this story?
    - a. bridge
    - b. rainwater
    - c. hole

4. Why does the mayor think the hole is dangerous?
    - a. Someone could fall into it.
    - b. It could get muddy.
    - c. It is full of dirt.

5. Which meaning of the word *bridge* is used in this story?
    - a. card game played by four people
    - b. the upper part of the nose
    - c. structure built across a body of water

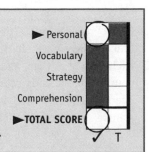

Add the numbers that you just checked to get your total score. (For example, if you checked 3, 2, 3, 2, and 1, your total score would be 11.) Fill in your score here. Then turn to page 203 and transfer your score onto Graph 1.

►Personal
Vocabulary
Strategy
Comprehension
►TOTAL SCORE

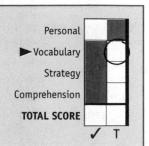

Check your answers with your teacher. Give yourself 1 point for each correct answer, and fill in your Vocabulary score here. Then turn to page 203 and transfer your score onto Graph 1.

Personal
►Vocabulary
Strategy
Comprehension
TOTAL SCORE

Strategy Check

Look back at the problem-solution frame that you created for the second half of "The Hole in the Road." Then answer these questions:

1. What is the result of filling the hole with soapsuds?
   a. The mayor disappears when he steps onto them.
   b. The hole gets nice and clean.
   c. The hole gets even deeper than before.

2. What solution do Daniel Daniel and the mayor try after filling the hole with soapsuds?
   a. filling the hole with rainwater
   b. digging up the hole
   c. building a bridge over the hole

3. What is the final solution, or end result?
   a. filling the hole with rainwater
   b. digging up the hole
   c. building a bridge over the hole

4. Why is the end result humorous?
   a. Much work is done, and the hole disappears.
   b. Much work is done, yet the hole remains.
   c. Much work is done, yet the people are still unhappy.

5. What would be the most sensible solution to the problem?
   a. putting a danger sign in front of the hole
   b. filling the hole with garbage
   c. filling the hole with more dirt

Comprehension Check

Review the story if necessary. Then answer these questions:

1. Why does the author describe the villagers as "silly people" in the first sentence of the story?
   a. to show that the story will be entertaining
   b. to show that the story will express her opinions
   c. to try to persuade readers to agree with her

2. Why is digging up the hole a silly solution?
   a. It takes too long.
   b. Digging is a lot of work.
   c. The more you dig, the deeper a hole gets.

3. Why are the people satisfied with the bridge?
   a. They think it solves the problem.
   b. They always wanted a bridge on the road.
   c. They don't want to hurt the mayor's feelings.

4. Why do people have to fill the hole with water once in a while?
   a. They think a bridge must go over water.
   b. It wouldn't be a hole if it didn't have water.
   c. People will not cross the bridge if there is no water.

5. What might the author be trying to say in an entertaining way?
   a. There are too many bridges in this world.
   b. Sometimes people try to solve easy problems with difficult solutions.
   c. Some problems just can't be solved.

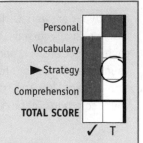
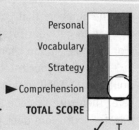

Extending

Choose one or both of these activities:

SOLVE PROBLEMS IN YOUR OWN TOWN

With a partner, look through some local newspapers and find a problem that your town has, such as potholes, graffiti, or speeding drivers. Find out what has been done to solve the problem. Then create a problem-solution frame to describe the problem, the solution or solutions that have been tried, and the results. If the problem has not been solved yet, add some solutions of your own to the chart, along with the results you'd expect.

TAKE A SURVEY

Record a classroom problem and list several ways to solve it. Then survey your classmates to see which solutions are most popular. (Make sure that each student votes only one time.) Display the results of your survey in a bar graph. You might use a computer software program to help you create the graph.

Resources

Books

Ketteman, Helen. *Bubba the Cowboy Prince: A Fractured Texas Tale.* Scholastic, 1997.

———. *Heat Wave.* Bt Bound, 2001.

———. *I Remember Papa.* Dial Books for Young Readers, 1998.

Laughter Is Good Medicine

ailing

cure

disease

germs

healing power

laughter

stress

workout

CLIPBOARD
Good Health

CLIPBOARD
Poor Health

Building Background

The title of the informational article you are about to read is actually an old saying: Laughter is good medicine. What is your opinion of this saying? Do you agree or disagree with it? Fill in the box below. Circle the word *agree* or *disagree* in the first line. Then write three reasons to support your opinion.

I agree/disagree that "laughter is good medicine" because:

1. _____

   _____

2. _____

   _____

3. _____

   _____

As you read the following article, look for details that support your opinion—or make you change your mind.

Vocabulary Builder

1. The words in the margin are all from the article "Laughter Is Good Medicine." Before you begin reading the article, decide which of the vocabulary words are related to good health and which are related to poor health. List each word on the appropriate clipboard.

2. As you read the article, look for other health-related words. Ask yourself if they are related to good health or poor health. If you can, add some of the words to the clipboards.

3. Save your work. You will use it again in the Vocabulary Check.

Strategy Builder

How to Read an Informational Article

- An **informational article** gives facts and details about a particular subject, or topic. Since the **topic** is what an article is all about, it is usually stated in the **title** of the article.

- Most informational articles are organized into **main ideas** and **supporting details**. These ideas and details help explain or support the topic.

- The main ideas are often stated in **headings** throughout the article. The supporting details are given in the paragraphs below the headings. The following example is from an informational article on smoking. The supporting details are underlined.

Smoking Is Bad for Your Health

Smoking Can Cause Diseases
When people smoke for many years, they increase their risk of certain diseases. For example, many smokers develop chronic bronchitis. *Chronic* means "constant." That means that people with chronic bronchitis have a constant cough and irritated lungs.
   Another disease that smokers can get is emphysema. This disease cannot be cured. People who have severe cases of emphysema must always have a supply of oxygen nearby because they have trouble breathing.

- If you wanted to highlight the topic, main idea, and supporting details in the example above, you could put them on a graphic organizer. Here is how they would look on a **concept map**, or web:

Laughter Is Good Medicine

As you read the beginning of this informational article, you can apply some of the strategies that you just learned. Notice the underlined phrases and sentences. They contain details that support the main idea in each heading. Can you tell what the topic of this article is? (Read the title for a hint.)

How many times a day do you laugh? Ten times a day? Five times? Or are you such a sad sack that you never laugh? If that's true, you need to lighten up. Scientists now say that laughing is good for your health.

Adults Laugh Less than Children Do

An adult laughs about 15 times a day. But most children laugh 50 times a day. Why? Because children spend much of their time having fun and doing silly things. They play—and they laugh.

Adults, though, are loaded down with real-life duties. They work all day. They pay bills and keep the car running. They have to do laundry and get the kids to school on time. In short, adults are busy. When do they have time to laugh?

Doctors say that adults should *make* time for fun. These experts have studied how feelings can change a person's health. They know that having fun is important. But getting patients to enjoy life is not easy, say the doctors. Adults don't place much value on play. Too often, having fun is seen as a waste of time.

Laughter as Treatment

In 1979, Norman Cousins wrote a book called *The Anatomy of an Illness.* It was about Cousins's fight with a deadly **disease**. He didn't want to stay in bed and feel sorry for himself. Instead, he tried to look on the bright side. He made **laughter** a part of his daily treatment.

Cousins's idea seemed to work. His health improved, and he felt better. He lived 12 years after he had first become ill. Other sick people followed his lead. They, too, tried to laugh through their pain. They hoped that a happy frame of mind *would* help heal an **ailing** body.

Proof that Laughter Heals

The claim that laughter can heal is not new. Some doctors held that belief as early as the 1300s. They saw a link between the health of the mind and that of the body. One such doctor was Henri de Mondeville. He thought that joy in his patients' lives would improve their health. He told the family and friends of his patients to "cheer them" and "tell them jokes."

Why is the **healing power** of laughter once again new today? We now have proof that laughter is good for the body! Until a few years ago, that idea was just a hunch. Thanks to Norman Cousins, doctors now have some hard facts about laughter. Cousins spent his last years studying laughter as medicine. He worked with doctors at the UCLA Medical Center to research humor. Together, Cousins and the doctors learned more about *how* laughter heals.

Doctors found that laughing gives more strength to the body's immune system. This system helps the body fight disease. The immune system contains "killer" cells. These cells try to kill harmful cells that enter the body. Laughter makes the job of the killer cells easier. When a person laughs, the body reacts. This reaction sends special chemicals all through the body. That action, in turn, readies the immune system to fight off **germs**.

 Stop here for the Strategy Break.

Strategy Break

If you were to create a concept map for the first part of this article, it might look like this:

Laughter Is Good Medicine

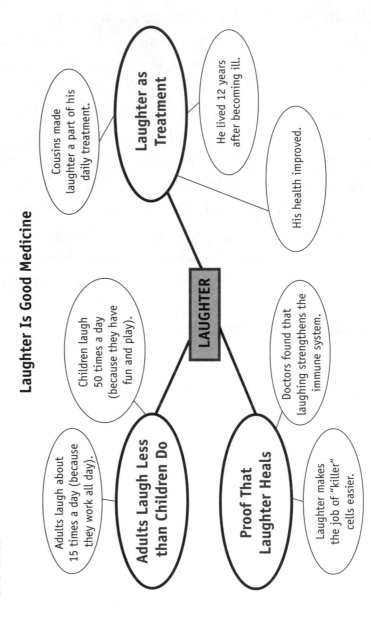

As you continue reading, keep looking for the main ideas and supporting details. At the end of this article, you will use some of them to create a concept map of your own.

Go on reading.

Laughter as Exercise

Think about how you feel after a good **workout**. You may be a bit sore and tired, but you feel wonderful. Long distance runners say that they even feel "high" after a few miles. Laughter has the same effect; it feels good to laugh.

Indeed, laughter is a kind of exercise. Think about your last big laugh. How did your body react? You threw back your head and took a deep breath. Blood rushed to your brain. Maybe you felt a little giddy. You were not worried about your homework or your next trip to the dentist. You could feel the stresses of daily life drain away.

What's more, your pulse rate and blood pressure went up as you laughed. Then they came down again and were lower than before you laughed. Cousins called laughter "internal jogging."

One study shows that 100 laughs do the body as much good as 10 minutes of rowing a boat. In other words, laughing gives the heart and lungs a good workout. In that sense, laughter is a bit like jogging—but without the sweat. This is the kind of workout you can enjoy while lying on the couch watching a funny TV show.

Shared Laughter

Annette Goodheart wrote a book on the power of laughter. She, too, says that humor can improve a person's health. She thinks that laughter may have the strongest effect on people in a group. When people laugh, they are in touch with themselves. Shared laughter makes people connect with each other. That's why laughter so often spreads to others in a group; it breaks through the feeling of being alone and apart from others.

Limits of Laughter

Goodheart warns that laughter is not a **cure**. It won't stop AIDS or the common cold. Yet it may help a person to heal, or feel better. Laughter offsets the **stress** caused by illness and worry. A sick person with reduced stress feels better in both body and spirit. Laughter can help a person heal. It can make even a dying person feel better.

No amount of laughter or medicine can keep a person from dying. But laughter is vital while we are alive. Fun and laughter do not just happen by themselves. You can look for reasons to have a good laugh each day. Unhappy people say that they can't laugh when they don't feel happy. "You have to make laughter a priority in life," Goodheart says. "You don't play when you feel better. You feel better when you play." ●

Strategy Follow-up

Now create a concept map for the section of this article called "Limits of Laughter."
The topic and main idea have been filled in for you.

Laughter Is Good Medicine

LAUGHTER

Limits of Laughter

✓ Personal Checklist

Read each question and put a check (✓) in the correct box.

1. In Building Background, you explained why you agree or disagree that "laughter is good medicine." How well were you able to find details in the article that supported your opinion or made you change your mind?
   - ☐ 3 (extremely well)
   - ☐ 2 (fairly well)
   - ☐ 1 (not well)

2. Before you read the article, how many vocabulary words were you able to put on the appropriate clipboards?
   - ☐ 3 (6–8 words)
   - ☐ 2 (3–5 words)
   - ☐ 1 (0–2 words)

3. In the Strategy Follow-up, how easily were you able to find the supporting details in "Limits of Laughter" and put them on your concept map?
   - ☐ 3 (extremely easily)
   - ☐ 2 (fairly easily)
   - ☐ 1 (not easily)

4. How well do you understand the information in this article?
   - ☐ 3 (extremely well)
   - ☐ 2 (fairly well)
   - ☐ 1 (not well)

5. Now that you've read the article, how easily would you be able to tell someone why "laughter is good medicine"?
   - ☐ 3 (extremely easily)
   - ☐ 2 (fairly easily)
   - ☐ 1 (not easily)

Vocabulary Check

Look back at the work you did in the Vocabulary Builder. Then answer each question by circling the correct letter.

1. How are laughter and a good workout both related to good health?
   - a. They both are a kind of exercise.
   - b. They both make you feel better.
   - c. Both of the above answers are correct.

2. According to the article, laughter helps fight stress. Which meaning of the word *stress* is the article using?
   - a. special emphasis or importance
   - b. tension or pressure on the mind and body
   - c. louder pronunciation of a particular syllable or word

3. Which of these words belongs on a list of words related to good health?
   - a. germs
   - b. cure
   - c. disease

4. Why would the word *ailing* belong on a list of words related to poor health?
   - a. *Ailing* means "ill."
   - b. *Ailing* means "getting better."
   - c. *Ailing* means "very healthy."

5. Which of the following is an example of the healing power of laughter?
   - a. Laughter strengthens the immune system.
   - b. Laughter makes people feel stressful.
   - c. Laughter cures the common cold.

Add the numbers that you just checked to get your Personal Checklist score. Fill in your score here. Then turn to page 203 and transfer your score onto Graph 1.

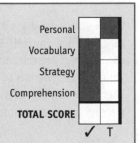

Check your answers with your teacher. Give yourself 1 point for each correct answer, and fill in your Vocabulary score here. Then turn to page 203 and transfer your score onto Graph 1.

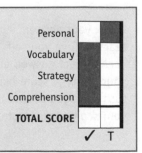

Strategy Check

Look back at the concept map that you created for "Limits of Laughter." Also review the article if necessary. Then answer these questions:

1. Which part of an informational article helps you best identify its topic?
   a. the title
   b. the headings
   c. the supporting details

2. Which word best describes what this article is all about?
   a. illness
   b. exercise
   c. laughter

3. Which detail describes one of the limits of laughter?
   a. Laughter is not a cure for AIDS or colds.
   b. Laughter can help a person heal.
   c. Laughter can make a dying person feel better.

4. Which main idea includes the detail that laughter has its strongest effect on people in groups?
   a. "Laughter as Exercise"
   b. "Shared Laughter"
   c. "Limits of Laughter"

5. If you were to create a concept map for "Laughter as Exercise," which of these supporting details would you include?
   a. Laughter is like "internal napping."
   b. Laughter is like "internal jogging."
   c. Laughter stresses the heart too much.

Comprehension Check

Review the article if necessary. Then answer these questions:

1. Why do children laugh more than adults?
   a. Adults work less.
   b. Children worry more.
   c. Children play more.

2. What do Norman Cousins, Henri de Mondeville, and Annette Goodheart have in common?
   a. They all wrote books on laughter.
   b. They all have said that laughter heals.
   c. They all lived during the 1300s.

3. Which of these statements is false?
   a. Doctors can cure any disease with laughter.
   b. Laughter helps the body fight disease.
   c. The idea that laughter can heal is not new.

4. Which of the following was *not* mentioned as a benefit of laughter?
   a. lowered blood pressure
   b. lowered pulse rate
   c. fewer muscle aches

5. How does laughter help the immune system?
   a. It tickles the "killer cells" and makes them laugh.
   b. It gets the "killer cells" ready to fight off germs.
   c. It sends germ chemicals all through the body.

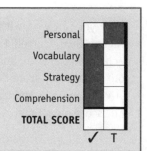

Check your answers with your teacher. Give yourself 1 point for each correct answer, and fill in your Strategy score here. Then turn to page 203 and transfer your score onto Graph 1.

Personal
Vocabulary
Strategy
Comprehension
TOTAL SCORE
✓ T

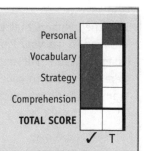

Check your answers with your teacher. Give yourself 1 point for each correct answer, and fill in your Comprehension score here. Then turn to page 203 and transfer your score onto Graph 1.

Personal
Vocabulary
Strategy
Comprehension
TOTAL SCORE
✓ T

Extending

Choose one or both of these activities:

MAKE A JOKE BOOK

How can you help heal the children in your local hospital? By making them laugh! Get together with a group of classmates and make a book of jokes, riddles, and funny stories. Use the resources listed on this page for help if you'd like. Illustrate the book with your own artwork or pictures from magazines. Find the phone number and address of your local hospital. Then ask your teacher to call and find out who should receive your book. Mail the book to that person, along with a letter asking him or her to share the book with the hospital's young patients.

RESEARCH NORMAN COUSINS

Find out more about how laughter helped Norman Cousins. Check several sources, including his book *The Anatomy of an Illness*, and see if you can find answers to some of the following questions. (If you have other questions, be sure to add them to the list.)

- What deadly disease did Norman Cousins have?

- What made him decide to try laughter as a treatment for his disease?

- What were some of his "treatments"?

- Were there some treatments that worked better than others?

- How did Cousins influence others with his ideas?

Resources

Books

Gallant, Morrie. *Awesome Riddle Book.* Sterling Publications, 1998.

O'Donnell, Rosie. *Kids Are Punny 2: More Jokes Sent by Kids to The Rosie O'Donnell Show.* Warner Books, 1998.

Pine, David J. *365 Good Health Hints.* Hay House, 1994.

Riccio, Nina M. *Five Kids and a Monkey Investigate a Vicious Virus.* Creative Attic, 1997.

Stamper, Genevieve, and Judith Stamper. *101 Wacky Computer Jokes.* Scholastic, 1998.

Web Sites

http://www.fitnessfever.com
This site offers tips for healthful eating, fitness games, and other tools to help you live a healthy life.

http://www.worldlaughtertour.com
This site suggests there are many ways to live longer through laughter.

Video/DVD

Chicken Fat—Youth Fitness Video. Kimbo, 1996.

The Visitor

Building Background

The story you are about to read is called "The Visitor." Think about the last time you had visitors staying at your house. How did you and your family get ready for their arrival? What chores did you do? What meals did you prepare? How did you feel before your visitors arrived? How did your pet feel? . . . Hmm. Now *that's* a strange question. But did you ever wonder how pets might feel when their owners have visitors?

The pet in "The Visitor" is a dog named Sandy. Author Katherine Ayres imagines what Sandy is thinking and feeling when his owners have visitors. As you read this story, think about Sandy's feelings. If you have a pet, could it ever feel the way Sandy does?

barked

bounded

dozed

galloped

greet

said

trudged

vacuum

wagged

waltzed

Vocabulary Builder

1. Before you begin reading "The Visitor," read the words in the margin. Which of the words describe things that dogs do? Write those words in the oval on the left. (If you don't know what a word means, look it up in a dictionary.)

2. Which of the words describe things that people do? Write those words in the oval on the right.

3. Which of the words describe things that both dogs *and* people do? Write those words in the center, where the ovals overlap.

4. Save your work. You will use it again in the Vocabulary Check.

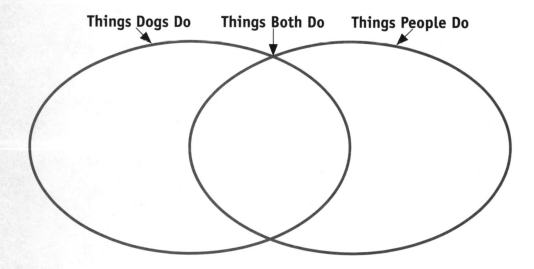

Things Dogs Do   **Things Both Do**   **Things People Do**

Strategy Builder

How to Follow the Sequence of a Story

- When you read a story, you are reading a series of events. These events happen in order, or **sequence**. Paying attention to the order of events will help you: (1) follow what is happening, (2) predict what might happen next, and (3) make sense of the story.

- To make the sequence of events as clear as possible, writers often use **signal words**. Some examples of signal words are *first, then, later, after lunch,* and *the next morning.*

- The following paragraph is from a story about a girl named Edie. See if you can use the underlined signal words to follow the sequence of events.

> One day Edie was walking through the park. She got tired after a while, so she sat down in the grass. It was a lovely day. Birds were singing, and there was a slight breeze. Suddenly a ball rolled in front of Edie. She didn't know where it had come from. It was bright red, with a yellow star. A moment later, a little boy came toward her. He was holding out his hand. His mother was walking behind him. Edie smiled at the boy while she handed him the ball.

- If you wanted to keep track of the main events in the paragraph above, you could organize them on a **sequence chain**. It would look like this:

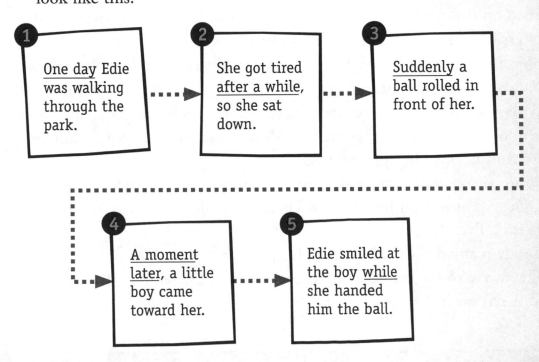

The Visitor

by Katherine Ayres

As you read the first half of "The Visitor," you can apply the strategies that you just learned. Notice the underlined signal words. They will give you a more exact picture of when things happened. (Don't forget to pay attention to what Sandy thinks and feels.)

Sandy **bounded** outside. Fresh air. Wide meadows. Shining mountains. New snow.

He **barked**. Two other dogs barked in answer. Ginger and Pepper ran to join him. They sniffed at an elk trail, but the scent was old. They waded through belly-deep snow and made round holes with their noses. They barked at a magpie who scolded from an aspen branch.

Then the yellow bus rattled up the road. Ginger and Pepper raced to **greet** their boys.

Sandy watched as his two friends herded their children home and disappeared indoors. With a drooping tail, he **trudged** back to his own house. His people were kind. But they walked, they didn't run. They didn't chase and burrow in the snowbanks.

A nasty scrubbing smell met him at the door. Noises came from the kitchen. The woman was up to something.

"Hi there, Sandy," Becky called. "Visitors coming today."

The smell in the kitchen made Sandy blink. He backed out and crept upstairs to wait until it went away. But upstairs the silver-haired man turned on the noisy machine. Sandy hated that machine even more than the terrible smell. He hid his head under the bed.

"Visitors coming, Sandy. Time to **vacuum** the rugs," Bill explained.

Sandy hid in the closet.

At last the machine was quiet. The scrubbing smell had gone, and wonderful odors come from the kitchen. Meat, bread, cookies. Sandy hurried in to find Becky. He yipped softly.

"You beggar, you," she **said**, scratching under his chin. "Here's a scrap."

Sandy went to find Bill. He was kneeling beside the hearth, stacking logs for a fire.

Sandy planted his head between his paws and **dozed**.

He awoke to the sound of a motor. Racing to the window, he looked out. A red car had stopped in the driveway.

Doors opened. People climbed out. They hauled suitcases to the house. The visitors were here!

Sandy **galloped** to the front door. He welcomed each visitor with a wet kiss. A man, a woman, a girl. A girl for him to play with!

"Down, Sandy," Becky said.

"No, Granny," said the girl. "It's all right. Sandy just wants to dance."

The girl took Sandy's paws and **waltzed** across the hall. Sandy licked her cheek. The girl giggled.

"You're staying up here, Rachel," Becky called. "Next to Grandpa and me. Your mother and father will stay downstairs."

"Where does Sandy sleep?"

"In our room," Becky explained. "He'll be next-door to you."

Sandy wasn't allowed to beg at dinnertime. But <u>when the people gathered to eat</u>, he crawled under the table. He looked around. Four pairs of big feet. One pair of small feet. He edged close to the small feet.

They rested on his strong back. A hand sneaked down with a bite of meat. Sandy nibbled and thumped his tail.

<u>After dinner</u> the people gathered beside the fire. The big people sat in chairs. The girl, Rachel, lay on the floor. Sandy lay beside her. He rolled on his back and wriggled. Rachel scratched his belly. He nipped her socks. She caught his front paws and shook both at once.

Too soon it was time for bed. Rachel kissed all the people good night and hugged Sandy. <u>When it was time for him to go to bed</u>, he padded into her room to say good night. Yes. She was safe.

 Stop here for the Strategy Break.

Strategy Break

Many things have happened in the story so far. If you were to create a sequence chain to put the main events in order, it might look like this:

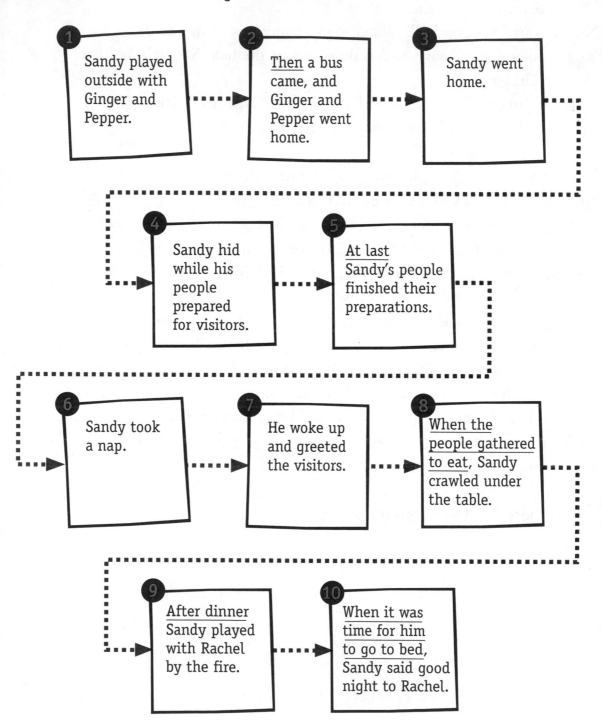

1. Sandy played outside with Ginger and Pepper.

2. Then a bus came, and Ginger and Pepper went home.

3. Sandy went home.

4. Sandy hid while his people prepared for visitors.

5. At last Sandy's people finished their preparations.

6. Sandy took a nap.

7. He woke up and greeted the visitors.

8. When the people gathered to eat, Sandy crawled under the table.

9. After dinner Sandy played with Rachel by the fire.

10. When it was time for him to go to bed, Sandy said good night to Rachel.

As you continue reading, keep paying attention to the sequence of events. Also, keep looking for signal words. At the end of the story, you will use some of them to create a sequence chain of your own.

Go on reading to see what happens.

At first light, Sandy nosed into the bedroom and kissed Rachel awake. After breakfast she put on her red snowsuit, and he took her out for a run. He showed her the wide meadow where elk had left fresh tracks. He led her to the aspen tree where a pair of magpies argued. She threw balls of snow, and Sandy caught them in midair.

"I love you, Sandy," she said, throwing her arms around his neck.

Sandy **wagged** his tail and licked her cold nose.

Every day they played, and every night Sandy sat by Rachel's feet at the table and said good night to the sleeping girl in her bed.

Finally, a morning came when the visitors loaded all their suitcases back into the car. They took coats out of the closet and wrapped themselves tight against the cold.

"Good-bye, Sandy," Rachel said. She ruffled the fur around his neck and gave him a big hug. Then she went out the front door.

All that day, Sandy guarded the door, just in case. When he went for a run, he didn't run far. He circled the house, looking for a red car.

At dinner, he crawled under the table, but only two pairs of feet showed. Big feet. And no fingers offered bits of anything. The visitors didn't come back that night. Sandy checked Rachel's room just to make sure. Empty.

The next morning, it was still empty. No one to kiss awake.

Sandy watched and waited for days, but no visitor came.

When Becky took the sheets off the bed in the bedroom, Sandy caught the girl's scent. But it was faint, almost like a memory.

He followed Becky like a shadow as she put new sheets on the girl's bed. He sat and watched as she scrubbed the bathroom. He tried not to mind the nasty smell. He glided down the steps and followed her into the hall. Then she opened the big closet.

Sandy took a look, and his tail began to wave like a flag in a stiff wind. There in the closet hung a snowsuit. It was too small for Bill or Becky. And it was red.

Sandy poked his nose into one of the snowsuit's legs. He caught the girl's smell. His tail flapped harder.

"Yes, Sandy. I miss her, too," Becky said. She patted his head. "But she'll be back. Your girl will come again to play." ●

Strategy Follow-up

Now create a sequence chain for the second half of "The Visitor." Some of the chain has been filled in for you.

1 At first light,

2 After breakfast

3 _____ they played, and _____ Sandy said good night to Rachel.

4 Finally,

5 At dinner,

6 The next morning,

7 Becky cleaned the house. _____ she opened the big closet.

8 Sandy caught Rachel's smell on the snowsuit and wagged his tail.

9 Becky told Sandy

✓Personal Checklist

Read each question and put a check (✓) in the correct box.

1. How well do you understand Sandy's thoughts and feelings in this story?
   - ☐ 3 (extremely well)
   - ☐ 2 (fairly well)
   - ☐ 1 (not well)

2. In the Vocabulary Builder, how easily were you able to put the vocabulary words on the Venn diagram?
   - ☐ 3 (extremely easily)
   - ☐ 2 (fairly easily)
   - ☐ 1 (not easily)

3. How well were you able to complete the sequence chain in the Strategy Follow-up?
   - ☐ 3 (extremely well)
   - ☐ 2 (fairly well)
   - ☐ 1 (not well)

4. How well do you understand why Sandy likes having Rachel for a visitor?
   - ☐ 3 (extremely well)
   - ☐ 2 (fairly well)
   - ☐ 1 (not well)

5. How well do you understand why Sandy gets so excited when he sees the red snowsuit in the closet?
   - ☐ 3 (extremely well)
   - ☐ 2 (fairly well)
   - ☐ 1 (not well)

Vocabulary Check

Look back at the work you did in the Vocabulary Builder. Then answer each question by circling the correct letter.

1. Which vocabulary word describes something that only a *dog* can do?
   - a. said
   - b. galloped
   - c. waltzed

2. Which vocabulary word describes something that only a *person* can do?
   - a. dozed
   - b. vacuum
   - c. trudged

3. Which phrase describes something that both dogs *and* people can do?
   - a. vacuum a dirty carpet
   - b. bark at an animal
   - c. bound down the stairs

4. A person might greet someone by saying, "Hello." How might a dog greet someone?
   - a. by wagging its tail
   - b. by waltzing to music
   - c. by saying, "Hello"

5. Which word is defined as "had all four feet off the ground in a single stride"?
   - a. waltzed
   - b. trudged
   - c. galloped

Add the numbers that you just checked to get your Personal Checklist score. Fill in your score here. Then turn to page 203 and transfer your score onto Graph 1.

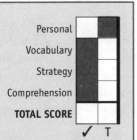

Check your answers with your teacher. Give yourself 1 point for each correct answer, and fill in your Vocabulary score here. Then turn to page 203 and transfer your score onto Graph 1.

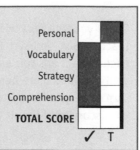

Strategy Check

Look back at the sequence chain you completed in the Strategy Follow-up. Then answer these questions:

1. Sandy wakes Rachel at first light. What time of day do the signal words *at first light* describe?
   a. sunrise
   b. midday
   c. sundown

2. What do Sandy and Rachel do every day?
   a. They sleep by the fire.
   b. They clean the house.
   c. They play outside.

3. What does Becky do before and after Rachel's visit?
   a. She cleans the house.
   b. She cooks extra food.
   c. She plays outside with Sandy.

4. When does Sandy see the red snowsuit in the closet?
   a. before Becky opens the closet door
   b. after Becky opens the closet door
   c. after Becky tells Sandy his girl will be back

5. Which sentence tells the main events of this story?
   a. The visitors arrive, leave for a while, and then return.
   b. The visitors arrive, stay a few days, and then leave.
   c. The visitors arrive, move in, and then leave for a while.

Comprehension Check

Review the story if necessary. Then answer these questions:

1. Who are the visitors in this story?
   a. Becky and Bill
   b. Rachel and her family
   c. Ginger and Pepper

2. Why is Sandy sad in the beginning?
   a. He hates the sound of the vacuum cleaner.
   b. His people are not kind to him.
   c. He has no one to play with in the snow.

3. Why does the author call Becky and Bill "Sandy's people"?
   a. She's calling them what Sandy would call them.
   b. That's what Bill and Becky call themselves.
   c. That's what the visitors call them.

4. How does Sandy feel at the end of the story?
   a. lonely
   b. afraid
   c. happy

5. Why does Sandy miss Rachel so much?
   a. He misses playing outside with Rachel.
   b. Rachel is one of Sandy's people.
   c. Sandy wants more food from the table.

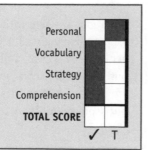

Check your answers with your teacher. Give yourself 1 point for each correct answer, and fill in your Strategy score here. Then turn to page 203 and transfer your score onto Graph 1.

Personal
Vocabulary
Strategy
Comprehension
TOTAL SCORE

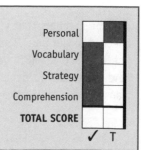

Check your answers with your teacher. Give yourself 1 point for each correct answer, and fill in your Comprehension score here. Then turn to page 203 and transfer your score onto Graph 1.

Personal
Vocabulary
Strategy
Comprehension
TOTAL SCORE

Extending

Choose one or both of these activities:

PET-CARE TIPS

Imagine you are the proud owner of a new puppy. Decide what kind of puppy it is, such as a poodle, a collie, or a German shepherd. Then make a poster showing what you will need to do to take care of your puppy. Include how much time you plan to spend feeding, walking, grooming, and playing with your puppy each day. Also include what you will feed it, as well as how often you will feed it. To get the information you need for your particular kind of puppy, consider talking to a pet-store owner or a veterinarian. Or check out some of the books or Web sites listed on this page.

WRITE ABOUT YOUR PET

Choose your own pet, or one that you would like to have, and write a story about it. Before you begin writing, brainstorm a list of words that tell how your pet moves, makes noises, and shows affection. Then imagine what your pet thinks and feels about a thing, a person, or an event. Try writing your story from your pet's point of view.

Resources

Books

American Kennel Club. *The Complete Dog Book for Kids.* Howell Book House, 1996.

Christopher, Matt. *The Dog That Called the Pitch.* Little, Brown, 1998.

Conrad, Pam. *Don't Go Near That Rabbit, Frank!* HarperCollins, 1998.

McMains, Joel M. *Dog Training Projects for Young People.* Howell Book House, 1995.

Web Sites

http://pets.yahoo.com
This site includes links to information about breeds and pet behavior.

http://www.healthypet.com
This site answers questions and gives advice about pet care.

Video/DVD

Dog. BBC Wildvision, 1994.

Dogs Who "Think"

Building Background

The article you are about to read is about work dogs, such as police dogs and guide dogs. What do you know about these dogs? Get together with your classmates and record your ideas on a concept map like the one below. When you finish reading, get together again and add more information to the concept map.

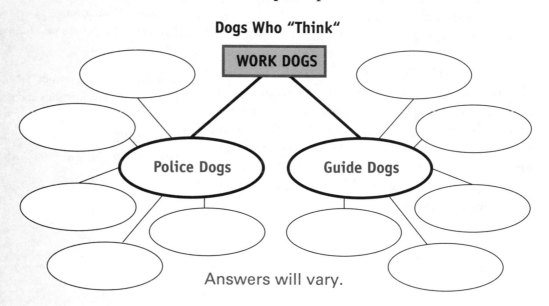

Dogs Who "Think"

WORK DOGS

Police Dogs   Guide Dogs

Answers will vary.

Vocabulary Builder

breeds

guide dogs

judgment

police dogs

search

traits

1. The questions below contain words from "Dogs Who 'Think.'" Before you begin reading the article, try to answer as many of the questions as possible. The vocabulary words are underlined.
   a. How do <u>guide dogs</u> help people?
   b. What kinds of <u>judgments</u> might guide dogs need to make?
   c. What <u>traits</u> do guide dogs and <u>police dogs</u> need?
   d. What <u>breed</u> of dog is most often chosen for police work?
   e. Why do police dogs need to learn how to <u>search</u>?

2. As you read the article, find the answers to these questions. If necessary, change or add to the answers you've already written.

3. Save your work. You will use it again in the Vocabulary Check.

Strategy Builder

How to Read an Informational Article

- In Lesson 2 you learned that an **informational article** gives facts and details about a topic. You also learned that an informational article is organized into **main ideas** and **supporting details**.

- Sometimes main ideas are stated in **headings** throughout an article. At other times, however, they are stated in sentences that come at the beginning of a paragraph or section. A **main idea sentence** sums up what a paragraph or section is about. The rest of the paragraph or section contains details that support, or tell more about, the main idea.

- The following example is from an informational article on an organization called Loving Paws. The main idea sentence is underlined once. Details that support the main idea are underlined twice.

Loving Paws Assistance Dogs

Loving Paws Assistance Dogs is an organization that trains dogs to help physically disabled children. Loving Paws was founded in 1994 and is a nonprofit organization. It trains dogs to help American children aged 18 years or younger. Loving Paws places most of its dogs with children who have spinal cord injuries. However, some of its dogs go to children with disabilities caused by muscular dystrophy, cerebral palsy, and spina bifida.

- If you wanted to show the main idea sentence and supporting details on a graphic organizer, you could put them on a **main idea table**. It would look like this:

Loving Paws Assistance Dogs

Main Idea Sentence: Loving Paws Assistance Dogs is an organization that trains dogs to help physically disabled children.				
Detail #1	**Detail #2**	**Detail #3**	**Detail #4**	**Detail #5**
founded in 1994	nonprofit organization	trains dogs to help American children aged 18 years or younger	places most of its dogs with children who have spinal cord injuries	some of its dogs go to children with disabilities caused by muscular dystrophy, cerebral palsy, and spina bifida

Dogs Who "Think"

As you read the beginning of this informational article, you can apply the strategies that you just learned. The main idea sentence in each section is underlined once. Supporting details are underlined twice.

*The saying "Dogs are people's best friends" is an old one. People and dogs have lived together since ancient times. Many dogs serve only as pets. But some dogs have real jobs to do. They work as **police dogs** and as **guide dogs** for the blind.*

*Some **breeds** of dog do these jobs better than others. Very often, people choose German shepherds for this work. What makes these dogs so good at it?*

The Right Stuff

German shepherds have many qualities that make them good work dogs. For one thing, they are the right size. They are quite large, and they are strong. With big chests, they can get enough wind for long runs. But their chests are not too big. So their steps stay steady when they walk and run.

German shepherds have a thick coat of fur that protects them in bad weather. It also helps them stay clean.

They look alert and are very smart. So it is easy to train them to do hard jobs.

What's more, German shepherds have the right **traits**. Most dogs tend to be loyal, good friends. But these dogs will do what it takes to please their owners. They are willing animals. They are patient and can wait quietly for a long time. The dogs' calm and gentle natures show that they can be well trained.

Poor Choices

Other dogs do not work out as well. A dachshund is not a good choice. It is not large enough for many jobs. And a dachshund does not have the right nature. Dachshunds are smart enough for training. But they like to avoid doing things they do want to do.

Another poor choice is a poodle. A poodle may be smarter than a German shepherd. It can train much faster than a shepherd dog. But poodles don't have good **judgment.** If a poodle led a blind person, it would do everything the person said. When that person said "Forward," the poodle would go forward, even if a car was coming! On the other hand, a German shepherd is not only glad to help people. This dog also knows when *not* to follow an order!

A German shepherd also has a lot of heart—the dog wants to be of help. Though tired or even hurt, a German shepherd will keep going.

 Stop here for the Strategy Break.

Strategy Break

If you were to stop and create a main idea table for the section of this article called "The Right Stuff," if might look like this:

The Right Stuff

Main Idea Sentence: German shepherds have many qualities that make them good work dogs.

Detail #1	Detail #2	Detail #3	Detail #4
They are the right size.	They have a thick coat of fur.	They are alert and smart.	They have the right traits.

As you continue reading, keep looking for main idea sentences and details. At the end of this article, you will use some of them to create a main idea table of your own.

 Go on reading.

Police Dog Training

Trainers work a long time to prepare police dogs for their work. They choose the dogs when they are still puppies. Police dogs train in a police barracks. But future guide dogs start their training another way. They live with a family for a year. In a home, they get used to being around all kinds of people.

When training starts, a police dog learns how to attack, but it only does so on command. First the dog bites a rag that the trainer waves in front of his own face. Then the dog practices on a person who wears thick arm pads. The dog learns to attack and hold on to someone. But the dog does not bite that person. Why not? Most of the time, police dogs don't have to attack. When people see police dogs coming, they give up. This is true even in prison fights.

Police dogs also learn to **search** for things. To teach this skill, a trainer first throws a stick for the dog to fetch. All dogs like to go after sticks. But a police dog learns to fetch other things too.

Next, the trainer lets the dog sniff an object. In this way, the dog learns the smell of the thing it is going to look for. Then the trainer hides the object far away. The dog must not see the trainer hide it. The dog then searches the area part by part. The dog's careful plan and keen sense of smell leave no spot unchecked. A dog can find almost anything by its smell.

On the Job

A trained German shepherd can find something even when it doesn't know what the object is. The trainer just says "Search," and the dog is on its way. It shows the trainer anything that seems out of place. Maybe a bank robber buried some loot. The dog finds any newly dug patches of dirt. The robber might be hiding. The dog walks right past other people and finds the one police want. If the dog is looking for a missing person, it starts at that person's home. Of all the foot tracks in the house, the dog must sniff out the freshest set.

Guide Dog Training

Like a police dog, a guide dog needs a lot of training. A guide dog must also use good judgment. The dog's "work clothes" for this job consist of a guide harness. In the harness, the dog learns to walk to the left and just ahead of the trainer. Outdoors, the dog must learn not only to steer clear of trees and people. It must also learn to give its owner room to avoid these things too.

A guide dog must guess ahead of time how high and wide things are. For example, an owner might be headed for a low tree branch. A well-trained dog can tell that the branch is too low in time to lead the owner around it.

The dog must know why it is being trained. Knowing this helps the dog act wisely when faced with a new problem. For example, a guide dog learns to stop at each curb when crossing a street. But just stopping is not enough if that stop also leads the owner into a ditch nearby. The dog must understand that the goal of training is to keep the owner safe. Then the dog makes the choices that protect the owner.

A Working Team

Training centers match guide dogs with blind persons. Just one blind person in ten can learn to use a guide dog. The person has to like dogs. He or she should also be willing to learn new ways to do everyday things. The dog and the new owner train together for about a month. Then the owner takes the dog to its new home. They will both start a new life as a working team.

It may be a pet, a police dog, or a guide dog. In many ways, a German shepherd shows that it is indeed a person's best friend. ●

Strategy Follow-up

Now create a main idea table for the section of this article called "Guide Dog Training." Some of the table has been filled in for you.

Guide Dog Training

Main Idea Sentence:

Detail #1	Detail #2	Detail #3	Detail #4
In the harness, the dog learns	Outdoors, the dog must learn	A guide dog must learn to guess	The dog must know why it is being trained. The goal is to

✓Personal Checklist

Read each question and put a check (✓) in the correct box.

1. How well do you understand why German shepherds make good work dogs?
   - ☐ 3 (extremely well)
   - ☐ 2 (fairly well)
   - ☐ 1 (not well)

2. In Building Background, how well were you able to fill in the concept map with information about police dogs and guide dogs?
   - ☐ 3 (extremely well)
   - ☐ 2 (fairly well)
   - ☐ 1 (not well)

3. How well were you able to identify the main idea sentences and supporting details in this article?
   - ☐ 3 (extremely well)
   - ☐ 2 (fairly well)
   - ☐ 1 (not well)

4. How well were you able to answer the questions in the Vocabulary Builder?
   - ☐ 3 (extremely well)
   - ☐ 2 (fairly well)
   - ☐ 1 (not well)

5. How well do you understand why this article is called "Dogs Who 'Think'"?
   - ☐ 3 (extremely well)
   - ☐ 2 (fairly well)
   - ☐ 1 (not well)

Vocabulary Check

Look back at the work you did in the Vocabulary Builder. Then answer each question by circling the correct letter.

1. Which words best describe a guide dog?
   a. guide, protector, leader
   b. guard, server, follower
   c. protector, server, follower

2. What would be considered good judgment by a guide dog?
   a. walking under low branches
   b. running into traffic
   c. stopping at a curb

3. Which of the following is *not* a breed of dog?
   a. German shepherd
   b. guide dog
   c. poodle

4. Which of the following are traits of a German shepherd?
   a. poor judgment, small, stupid
   b. lazy nature, small, thick coat of fur
   c. smart, loyal, patient

5. Which sense does a police dog use when it searches for an object?
   a. its sense of taste
   b. its sense of smell
   c. its sense of hearing

Add the numbers that you just checked to get your Personal Checklist score. Fill in your score here. Then turn to page 203 and transfer your score onto Graph 1.

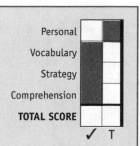

Check your answers with your teacher. Give yourself 1 point for each correct answer, and fill in your Vocabulary score here. Then turn to page 203 and transfer your score onto Graph 1.

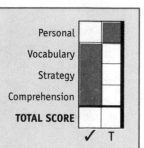

Strategy Check

Look back at the main idea table that you created for "Guide Dog Training." Also review the article. Then answer these questions:

1. Which details do *not* support the main idea of "The Right Stuff"?
   a. German shepherds are easy to train.
   b. German shepherds have calm, gentle natures.
   c. German shepherds have better judgment than poodles.

2. Which detail tells why dachshunds don't make good work dogs?
   a. They avoid doing things they don't want to do.
   b. They don't have good judgment.
   c. They know when *not* to follow an order.

3. Which section has the main idea sentence "Like a police dog, a guide dog needs a lot of training"?
   a. Guide Dog Training
   b. Poor Choices
   c. On the Job

4. Which is a detail from the section "A Working Team"?
   a. Dachshunds are smart enough for training.
   b. Just one blind person in ten can learn to use a guide dog.
   c. A poodle may be smarter than a German shepherd.

5. If you were to create a main idea table for "Police Dog Training," what would be your main idea sentence?
   a. Training centers match guide dogs with blind persons.
   b. Trainers work a long time to prepare police dogs for their work.
   c. Other dogs do not work out as well.

Comprehension Check

Review the article if necessary. Then answer these questions:

1. Which is an example of a dog that "thinks"?
   a. a dog that follows all of its owner's commands
   b. a dog that keeps its owner from walking into traffic
   c. a dog that is friendly and loyal to its owner

2. Why must guide dogs be good thinkers?
   a. so they can choose their owners wisely
   b. so they can track down and attack criminals
   c. so they can make choices that protect their owners

3. What important job does a police dog learn?
   a. to search for things
   b. to steer clear of things
   d. to guess how wide things are

4. When police dogs search for things, what do they look for?
   a. sticks that criminals have thrown
   b. anything that seems out of place
   c. holes where robbers bury themselves

5. Why do so few blind people have guide dogs?
   a. They must make the dogs do things their way.
   b. Most dogs want to be police dogs.
   c. They have to like dogs.

Check your answers with your teacher. Give yourself 1 point for each correct answer, and fill in your Strategy score here. Then turn to page 203 and transfer your score onto Graph 1.

Personal
Vocabulary
Strategy
Comprehension

TOTAL SCORE

✓ T

Check your answers with your teacher. Give yourself 1 point for each correct answer, and fill in your Comprehension score here. Then turn to page 203 and transfer your score onto Graph 1.

Personal
Vocabulary
Strategy
Comprehension

TOTAL SCORE

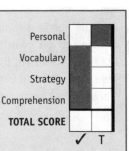

✓ T

Extending

Choose one or both of these activities:

WRITE A DOG'S JOURNAL ENTRY

Imagine you are a police dog or a guide dog. Using the resources listed on this page or information that you learned from this article, write a journal entry that describes a day in your life. Be sure to mention your trainer or owner and what you did to help him or her.

RESEARCH DOG TRAINING

Find out more about training a dog to assist people with special needs, to do police work, or to do tricks. Choose a task, such as learning to stop for a curb, learning to search, or learning to give you its paw. Then make a list of the steps you would take to train a dog to learn the task. Include the rewards and the number of trials you expect before the dog might be able to do the task regularly.

Resources

Books

Calmenson, Stephanie. *Rosie: A Visiting Dog's Story.* Houghton Mifflin, 1998.

Emert, Phyllis Raybin. *Guide Dogs.* Working Dogs. Crestwood House, 1985.

George, Charles. *Police Dogs.* Dogs at Work. Capstone Press, 1998.

Web Sites

http://www.guidedogs.com
This is the Web site of Guide Dogs for the Blind.

http://www.lovingpaws.com
This is the Web site of Loving Paws Assistance Dogs, which trains dogs to assist physically disabled children.

LESSON ⑤ Wagon Wheels

free land

prairie

winter

dugout

hungry

supply train

saddlebag

feast

Osage Indians

Building Background

Historical fiction tells a story based on real historical events. The story you are about to read is from a historical-fiction book called *Wagon Wheels*. The events in *Wagon Wheels* are based on the true story of the Muldie family. In 1878, the Muldies left their home in Kentucky and set out for Kansas. They were moving because they had heard about the Homestead Act. This act promised free land to anyone who was willing to settle in the West. The Muldies were among thousands of black pioneers who took advantage of this opportunity. The town the Muldies settled in was a black community called Nicodemus. It was named after a famous slave.

CLIPBOARD

free land

prairie

winter

dugout

hungry

Vocabulary Builder

1. The words and phrases in the margin are from the story you are about to read. On the clipboards, write a meaning for each word or phrase. (Use a dictionary, if necessary.) If a word or phrase has more than one meaning, predict how it might be used in the story and use that meaning.

2. On the lines below, predict what might happen in this story. Try to use all of the vocabulary words and phrases in your prediction.

3. Save your work. You will use it again in the Vocabulary Check.

CLIPBOARD

supply train

saddlebag

feast

Osage Indians

Strategy Builder

Drawing Conclusions While Reading a Story

- A **conclusion** is a decision that you reach after thinking about certain facts or information. When you read a story, you often draw conclusions based on information that the author gives you about the characters, setting, and events.

- Since historical fiction is based on things that really happened in the past, the **setting** and **characters** play an important role. You can use information about the setting and characters to draw conclusions about what things were like during the time a story takes place.

- Read the following paragraphs from *Wagon Wheels*. See if you can draw any conclusions about what life was like on the prairie during the late 1800s.

> We went to the river, and we followed the map. We walked all day. When Little Brother got tired, I carried him.
>
> At night we stopped and made a fire. I told Willie, "We will take turns. First I will watch the fire and you sleep. Fire the gun sometimes. It will scare wild animals away."
>
> There were plenty of wild animals on the prairie. Wolves. Panthers. Coyotes. Each night our fire and the sound of the gun kept them away.

- After reading these paragraphs, what conclusions can you draw about life on the prairie? Here are some conclusions that one reader drew:

"By reading these paragraphs, I can draw some conclusions about what life was like on the prairie. First, I can conclude that the prairie was very large because Willie and his brother needed a map to cross it. Also, they had been traveling for days, and they still hadn't gotten to where they were going. Next, I can conclude that the prairie was dangerous because it was filled with wolves, panthers, and coyotes—animals that can hurt or kill people. If these animals weren't dangerous, Willie and his brother wouldn't have had to take turns staying awake all night to watch for them. They also wouldn't have had to make fires and shoot guns to keep the animals away."

Wagon Wheels

by Barbara Brenner

As you read the first part of this story, see what conclusions you can draw about the characters and setting. Pay attention to the information that the author gives you to help you draw your conclusions.

"There it is, boys," Daddy said. "Across this river is Nicodemus, Kansas. That is where we arc going to build our house. There is **free land** for everyone here in the West. All we have to do is go and get it."

We had come a long way to get to Kansas. All the way from Kentucky. It had been a hard trip, and a sad one. Mama died on the way. Now there were just the four of us—Daddy, Willie, Little Brother, and me.

"Come on, boys," Daddy called. "Let's put our feet on free dirt."

We crossed the river, wagon and all.

A man was waiting for us on the other side. "I am Sam Hickman," he said. "Welcome to the town of Nicodemus."

"Why, thank you, Brother," Daddy said. "But where *is* your town?"

"Right here," Mr. Hickman said. We did not see any houses. But we saw smoke coming out of holes in the **prairie.**

"Shucks!" my daddy said. "Holes in the ground are for rabbits and snakes, not for free black people. I am a carpenter. I can build fine wood houses for this town."

"No time to build wood houses now," Mr. Hickman told my daddy. "**Winter** is coming. And winter in Kansas is *mean.* Better get yourself a **dugout** before the ground freezes."

Daddy knew Sam Hickman was right. We got our shovels and we dug us a dugout. It wasn't much of a place—dirt floor, dirt walls, no windows. And the roof was just grass and branches. But we were glad to have that dugout when the wind began to whistle across the prairie.

Every night Willie lit the lamp and made a fire. I cooked rabbit stew or fried a pan of fish fresh from the river.

After supper Daddy would always say, "How about a song or two?" He would take out his banjo and *Plink-a-plunk! Plink-a-plunk!*

Pretty soon that dugout felt like home.

 Stop here for the Strategy Break.

Strategy Break

What conclusions can you draw about this story so far? Using information from the story and what you learned in Building Background, try to answer the following questions. The hints below each question will help you draw your conclusions.

1. Why is Daddy so happy to see free land?
   Hint: Remember what you learned in Building Background about the Homestead Act.

   _____

   _____

2. Why do Daddy and the boys build a dugout rather than a wooden house?
   Hint: Think about what Mr. Hickman said, what you know about winter on the prairie, and how long it takes to build a wooden house.

   _____

   _____

3. What kind of person is Daddy?
   Hint: Think about what he says to his boys and Mr. Hickman.

   _____

   _____

As you continue reading, keep paying attention to the information that the author gives you about the characters and setting. At the end of the story, you will be asked to draw more conclusions.

 Go on reading to see what happens.

Winter came. And that Kansas winter *was* mean. It snowed day after day. We could not hunt or fish. We had no more rabbit stew. No more fish fresh from the river. All we had was cornmeal mush to eat.

Then one day there was no more cornmeal. There was not a lick of food in the whole town of Nicodemus. And nothing left to burn for firewood. Little Brother cried all the time—he was so cold and **hungry.**

Daddy wrapped blankets around him. "Hush, baby son," he said to him. "Try to sleep. **Supply train** will be coming soon." But the supply train did not come. Not that day or the next.

On the third day we heard the sound of horses. Daddy looked out to see who it was. "Oh Lord!" he said. "Indians!"

We were *so* scared. We had all heard stories about Indians. I tried to be brave. "I will get my gun, Daddy," I said.

But Daddy said, "Hold on, Johnny. Wait and see what they do."

We watched from the dugout. Everyone in Nicodemus was watching the Indians. First they made a circle. Then each Indian took something from his **saddlebag** and dropped it on the ground. The Indians turned and rode straight toward the dugouts.

"Now they are coming for us!" Willie cried.

We raised our guns. But the Indians rode right past us and kept going. We waited a long time to be sure they were gone. Then everyone ran out into the snow to see what the Indians had left. It was FOOD!

Everyone talked at once.

"Look!"

"Fresh deer meat!"

"Fish!"

"Dried beans and squash!"

"And bundles of sticks to keep our fires burning."

There was a **feast** in Nicodemus that night. But before we ate, Daddy said to us, "Johnny. Willie. Little Brother. I want you to remember this day. When someone says bad things about Indians, tell them the **Osage Indians** saved our lives in Nicodemus." ●

Strategy Follow-up

Use the information in the story to help you answer these questions:
1. The settlers in Nicodemus run out of food and firewood. What does this help you conclude about their knowledge of winter on the prairie?

_____

_____

2. Daddy and the boys get scared when the Indians arrive. What does this help you conclude about the stories they have heard about Indians?

_____

_____

3. Daddy tells the boys to "remember this day." What does this help you conclude about his feelings toward the Indians at the end of the story?

_____

_____

✓Personal Checklist

Read each question and put a check (✓) in the correct box.

1. How well do you understand why the Muldie family moved to Kansas?
   - ☐ 3 (extremely well)
   - ☐ 2 (fairly well)
   - ☐ 1 (not well)

2. How well were you able to use the vocabulary words to predict what might happen in the story?
   - ☐ 3 (extremely well)
   - ☐ 2 (fairly well)
   - ☐ 1 (not well)

3. How well do you understand why Daddy and the boys are afraid when the Indians come?
   - ☐ 3 (extremely well)
   - ☐ 2 (fairly well)
   - ☐ 1 (not well)

4. How well do you understand why the Indians give the settlers food?
   - ☐ 3 (extremely well)
   - ☐ 2 (fairly well)
   - ☐ 1 (not well)

5. How well do you understand why Daddy wants to tell people that the Osage Indians saved their lives?
   - ☐ 3 (extremely well)
   - ☐ 2 (fairly well)
   - ☐ 1 (not well)

Vocabulary Check

Look back at the work you did in the Vocabulary Builder. Then answer each question by circling the correct letter.

1. Which words best describe a prairie?
   a. tall mountains, many trees
   b. deep valleys, flowing rivers
   c. flat lands, few trees

2. Which word best describes winter on a prairie?
   a. harsh
   b. mild
   c. pleasant

3. Which meaning of the word *dugout* is used in this story?
   a. boat made by hollowing out a log
   b. rough shelter used for protection
   c. shelter at the side of a baseball field

4. What things might have been coming on the supply train?
   a. carpenters and Indians
   b. food and firewood
   c. horses and saddlebags

5. Which meaning of the word *feast* is used in this story?
   a. religious celebration
   b. thing that gives joy
   c. large, fancy meal

Add the numbers that you just checked to get your Personal Checklist score. Fill in your score here. Then turn to page 203 and transfer your score onto Graph 1.

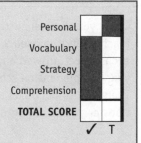

Check your answers with your teacher. Give yourself 1 point for each correct answer, and fill in your Vocabulary score here. Then turn to page 203 and transfer your score onto Graph 1.

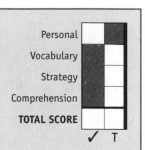

Strategy Check

Think about the information that the author gave you in this story. Use that information to help you answer these questions:

1. Daddy sings and plays his banjo. What can you conclude from his actions?
   a. He's trying to make the dugout feel like home.
   b. He doesn't feel like hunting and fishing.
   c. He's trying to make the boys leave the dugout.

2. What is the most likely reason for why the supply train doesn't come?
   a. The bad weather slowed it down.
   b. It took the wrong route and is lost.
   c. There is no supply train.

3. The settlers run out of food, but the Indians don't. What can you conclude from this fact?
   a. The Indians know how to prepare for winter.
   b. The Indians want to trade with the settlers.
   c. The Indians are very greedy.

4. Based on their actions toward the settlers, what conclusion can you draw about the Indians?
   a. They are trying to harm the settlers.
   b. They are trying to help the settlers.
   c. They are trying to trick the settlers.

5. Based on Daddy's words at the end of the story, which statement might he make?
   a. "The stories you hear about people are always true."
   b. "The stories you hear about people are not always true."
   c. "The stories you hear about people are never true."

Comprehension Check

Review the story if necessary. Then answer these questions:

1. Why does Daddy bring his family to Kansas?
   a. He wants to go where it is warmer.
   b. He wants to get free land.
   c. He wants to escape slavery.

2. Why had the trip to Kansas been a hard and sad one?
   a. The horse didn't want to cross the river.
   b. The boys' Mama died on the way.
   c. The family had all boys.

3. Why do Daddy and the boys dig a dugout?
   a. to protect themselves from winter
   b. to fit in with the rest of their neighbors
   c. to keep Mr. Hickman from getting angry

4. Daddy tells Johnny not to get his gun right away. What does this tell you about Daddy?
   a. He acts quickly without thinking first.
   b. He acts slowly without thinking first.
   c. He thinks carefully first before acting.

5. Why does Daddy tell the boys to "remember this day"?
   a. The feast was delicious.
   b. The Indians saved their lives.
   c. It was Daddy's birthday.

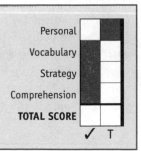

Check your answers with your teacher. Give yourself 1 point for each correct answer, and fill in your Strategy score here. Then turn to page 203 and transfer your score onto Graph 1.

Personal
Vocabulary
Strategy
Comprehension
TOTAL SCORE
✓ T

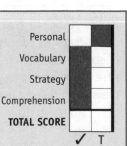

Check your answers with your teacher. Give yourself 1 point for each correct answer, and fill in your Comprehension score here. Then turn to page 203 and transfer your score onto Graph 1.

Personal
Vocabulary
Strategy
Comprehension
TOTAL SCORE
✓ T

Extending

Choose one or both of these activities:

RESEARCH MUSIC OF THE LATE 1800s

Daddy liked to play his banjo and sing. What songs might he have played? Find out what kinds of music were popular in America during the late 1800s. You can start by looking for the recordings listed on this page. Or you can search the Internet. Play some of the songs that you find for the rest of your class. Discuss why these songs might have been popular back then.

ROLE-PLAY A CONVERSATION

What if Daddy and the Osage Indians had had a conversation that day? What might they have said? Imagine that Daddy went out and talked to the Indians while they were dropping off the food. With a small group of classmates, role-play their conversation. Be sure to have the Indians explain why they are there and what they are doing. Have Daddy explain how he feels about what the Indians are doing.

Resources

Books

American Folksongs and Spirituals. Hal Leonard Publishing Corporation, 1996.

Brenner, Barbara. *On the Frontier with Mr. Audubon.* Boyds Mills Press, 1997.

Hamilton, Virginia. *Her Stories.* Blue Sky Press, 1995.

Turner, Ann, and Ronald Himler (illustrator). *Dakota Dugout.* Aladdin Paperbacks, 1989.

Wilson, Terry P. *The Osage.* Indians of North America. Chelsea House Publishers, 1988.

Web Sites

http://www.creativefolk.com/blackhistory.html
This Web site has links to photos, videos, books, and other resources for African American studies.

http://www.search.eb.com/blackhistory
This is *Encyclopaedia Britannica*'s online guide to Black history.

Audio Recordings

Holt, David. *I Got a Bullfrog: Folksongs for the Fun of It.* High Windy Audio, 2000.

Wade in the Water, Vol. 1: African American Spirituals—The Concert Tradition. Smithsonian Folkways, 1994.

Learning New Words

VOCABULARY

From Lesson 1
- soapsuds
- rainwater

From Lesson 2
- workout

From Lesson 5
- dugout
- saddlebag

Compound Words

A compound word is made of two words put together. In the story *Wagon Wheels,* the Indians take things from their saddlebags and leave them for the settlers. A *saddlebag* is a bag that hangs across a horse's back, just behind the saddle.

Fill in each blank with a compound word by combining a word from Row 1 with a word from Row 2.

Row 1:   tooth   wrist   basket   week   count

Row 2:   ache   down   watch   ball   end

1. Saturday and Sunday = _____

2. clock that is worn on the arm = _____

3. the calling of time before a launch = _____

4. game played with two net goals = _____

5. mouth pain caused by a cavity = _____

Suffixes

From Lesson 4
- judgment

A suffix is a word part that is added to the end of a word. When you add a suffix, you often change the word's meaning and function. For example, adding the suffix *-less* to the word *pain* changes the noun *pain* to an adjective meaning "without pain."

-ment

The suffix *-ment* is a special kind of suffix. It turns a word into a noun that means "the process or result of _____." In "Dogs Who 'Think,'" you learned that guide dogs must make good judgments. A *judgment* is the act or result of judging something.

Write the word that describes each situation below.

management   assignment   settlement   movement   announcement

1. the process of moving   _____

2. the result of assigning something   _____

3. the result of announcing something   _____

4. the process of managing   _____

5. the result of settling something   _____

Multiple-Meaning Words

A single word can have more than one meaning. For example, the word *bridge* can mean "a card game" or "a part of the nose" or "a structure built across water." To figure out which meaning of *bridge* an author is using, you have to use context. Context is the information surrounding a word that helps you understand its meaning. When you read "The Hole in the Road," you used context to figure out that the meaning the author is using for the word *bridge* is "a structure built across water."

Use context to figure out the correct meaning of each underlined word. Circle the letter of the correct meaning.

1. The radio announcer spoke in a very <u>deep</u> voice.

   a. hard to understand

   b. low in pitch

2. I see a huge <u>hole</u> in your argument.

   a. flaw or defect

   b. hollow place

3. Mother <u>cured</u> the fish so we could eat it later.

   a. preserved by salting

   b. brought back to health

4. <u>Stress</u> the second syllable when you say the word *remote*.

   a. add tension to

   b. add emphasis to

5. Passover is a <u>feast</u> that is celebrated by Jews.

   a. religious celebration

   b. large, fancy meal

VOCABULARY

From Lesson 1
- deep
- hole
- bridge

From Lesson 2
- cure
- stress

From Lesson 5
- feast

LESSON **6** Grandaddy's Place

Building Background

The story you are about to read is from a book called *Grandaddy's Place.* The girl in the story, Janetta, visits her grandfather's farm for the first time. Think about the first time you visited someplace new. Then answer the following questions:

- What new place did you visit? _____
- What were your first impressions of the place? _____
  _____
- Did your feelings change after you were there awhile? _____
- If so, in what ways? _____
- How do you feel about that place today, and why? _____
  _____
  _____

Vocabulary Builder

scared

shy

surprised

thoughtful

1. The vocabulary words in the margin are from *Grandaddy's Place.* They describe ways that people feel.

2. For each word, create a word map like the example below. (You will need to use your own paper.) Then try to predict how each word might be used in this story.

3. Save your work. You will use it again in the Vocabulary Check.

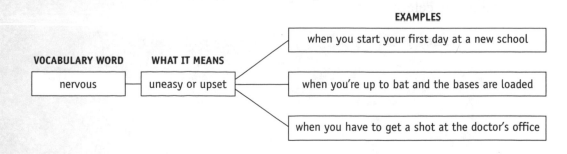

EXAMPLES

VOCABULARY WORD	WHAT IT MEANS	EXAMPLES
nervous	uneasy or upset	when you start your first day at a new school
		when you're up to bat and the bases are loaded
		when you have to get a shot at the doctor's office

Strategy Builder

Drawing Conclusions About Characters

- Remember that a **conclusion** is a decision you reach after thinking about information that the author gives you. You can draw conclusions about **characters** by looking at what they say, do, think, and feel.

- In many stories, the characters change in some way. As you read the paragraphs below, notice how Alex changes. See if you can draw any conclusions about him based on what he says and does.

Alex loves to sleep late when he's on vacation at his grandparents' house. So he wasn't very excited when Grandpa woke him before breakfast, just to go fishing. He rolled out of bed and into his sweats and climbed into the creaky, wooden rowboat.

Once they got to Grandpa's favorite spot, Alex yawned and refused to put even one disgusting old worm on his hook. But Grandpa helped him out and chuckled as he threaded the wriggly worm. Bored and tired, Alex sat waiting for something to happen.

Suddenly the pole jerked out of Alex's hands. "Reel it in, Alex!" Grandpa shouted. "You must have caught a northern. They love to give a good fight!"

After pulling and reeling and rocking the boat, Alex got the long, sleek northern close enough for Grandpa to snag its slapping, jerking body with a net.

"That was incredible! What a keeper!" Alex exclaimed excitedly. "Let's get him off the hook so I can catch another one. Grandpa, send over the worms. I've got another fish to catch!"

- If you wanted to track the changes in Alex's character, you could record them on a **character wheel** like the one below. (Notice the conclusions that one reader drew about Alex. They are in parentheses.)

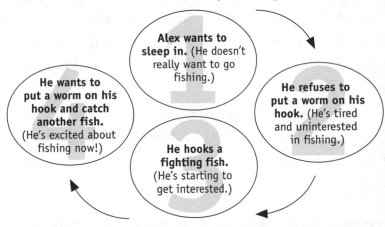

Grandaddy's Place

by Helen V. Griffith

As you read the first part of this story, notice what Janetta says, does, thinks, and feels. What conclusions can you draw about her?

One day Momma said to Janetta, "It's time you knew your grandaddy." Momma and Janetta went to the railroad station and got on a train. Janetta had never ridden on a train before. It was a long ride, but she liked it. She liked hearing about Momma's growing-up days as they rode along. She didn't even mind sitting up all night.

But when they got to Grandaddy's place, Janetta didn't like it at all.

The house was old and small. The yard was mostly bare red dirt. There was a broken-down shed and a broken-down fence.

"I don't want to stay here," said Janetta.

Momma said, "This is where I grew up."

An old man came out onto the porch.

"Say hello to your grandaddy," Momma said. Janetta was too **shy** to say hello. "You hear me, Janetta?" Momma asked.

"Let her be," said Grandaddy.

So Momma just said, "Stay out here and play while I visit with your grandaddy."

They left Janetta standing on the porch. She didn't know what to do. She had never been in the country before. She thought she might sit on the porch, but there was a mean-looking cat on the only chair. She thought she might sit on the steps, but there was a wasps' nest up under the roof. The wasps looked meaner than the cat. Some chickens were taking a dust-bath in the yard. When Janetta came near, they made mean sounds at her.

Janetta walked away. She watched the ground for bugs and snakes. All at once a giant animal came out of the broken-down shed. It came straight toward Janetta, and it was moving fast. Janetta turned and ran. She ran past the chickens and the wasps' nest and the mean-looking cat.

She ran into the house.

"There's a giant animal out there," she said.

Grandaddy looked **surprised**. "First I knew of it," he said.

"It has long legs and long ears and a real long nose," said Janetta.

Momma laughed. "Sounds like the mule," she said.

"Could be," said Grandaddy. "That mule's a tall mule."

"It chased me," said Janetta.

"It won't hurt you," Momma said. "Go back outside and make friends."

But Janetta wouldn't go back outside.

"Nothing out there likes me," she said.

 Stop here for the Strategy Break.

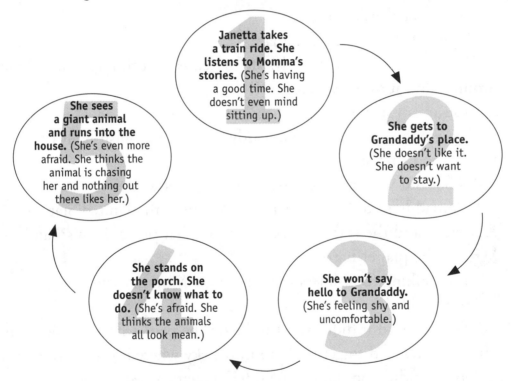

Strategy Break

What conclusions can you draw about Janetta? How has she changed so far?
If you were to begin a character wheel for Janetta, it might look this:

Janetta takes a train ride. She listens to Momma's stories. (She's having a good time. She doesn't even mind sitting up.)

She gets to Grandaddy's place. (She doesn't like it. She doesn't want to stay.)

She won't say hello to Grandaddy. (She's feeling shy and uncomfortable.)

She stands on the porch. She doesn't know what to do. (She's afraid. She thinks the animals all look mean.)

She sees a giant animal and runs into the house. (She's even more afraid. She thinks the animal is chasing her and nothing out there likes her.)

As you continue reading, keep noticing what Janetta says, does, thinks, and feels.
At the end of the story, you will finish Janetta's character wheel. Do her feelings
continue to change?

Go on reading to see what happens.

After dark Momma and Grandaddy and Janetta sat out on the steps. The mean-looking cat wasn't anywhere around. Janetta hoped the wasps were asleep. She was beginning to feel sleepy herself. Then a terrible sound from the woods brought her wide awake.

"Was that the mule?" she asked.

"That was just an old hoot owl singing his song," said Grandaddy.

"It didn't sound like singing to me," said Janetta.

"If you were an owl, you'd be tapping your feet," said Grandaddy.

They sat and listened to the owl, and then Grandaddy said, "It was just this kind of night when the star fell into the yard."

"What star?" asked Janetta.

"Now, Daddy," said Momma.

"It's a fact," said Grandaddy. "It landed with a thump, and it looked all around, and it said, 'Where am I?' "

"You mean stars speak English?" asked Janetta.

"I guess they do," said Grandaddy, "because English is all I know, and I understood that star just fine."

"What did you say to the star?" asked Janetta.

Grandaddy said, "I told that star, 'You're in the United States of America,' and the star said, 'No, I mean what planet is this?' and I said, 'This is the planet Earth.' "

"Stop talking foolishness to that child," Momma said.

"What did the star say?" asked Janetta.

"The star said it didn't want to be on the planet Earth," said Grandaddy. "It said it wanted to get back up in the sky where it came from."

"So what did you do, Grandaddy?" Janetta asked.

"Nothing," said Grandaddy, "because just then the star saw my old mule."

"Was the star **scared**?" Janetta asked.

"Not a bit," said Grandaddy. "The star said, 'Can that mule jump?' and I said, 'Fair, for a mule,' and the star said, 'Good enough.' Then the star hopped up on the mule's back and said, 'Jump.' "

Momma said, "Now, you just stop that talk."

"Don't stop, Grandaddy," said Janetta.

"Well," Grandaddy said, "the mule jumped, and when they were high enough up the star hopped off and the mule came back down again."

"Was the mule all right?" asked Janetta.

"It was **thoughtful** for a few days, that's all," said Grandaddy.

Janetta stared up at the sky. "Which star was it, Grandaddy?" she asked.

"Now, Janetta," Momma said, "you know that's a made-up story."

Grandaddy looked up at the stars. "I used to know," he said, "but I'm not sure anymore."

"I bet the mule remembers," Janetta said.

"It very likely does," said Grandaddy.

From somewhere in the bushes some cats began to yowl. "That's just the worst sound I know," Momma said. "Janetta, chase those cats."

"They're just singing their songs," said Grandaddy.

"That's right, Momma," said Janetta. "If you were a cat, you'd be tapping your feet."

Momma laughed and shook her head. "One of you is as bad as the other," she said. ●

Strategy Follow-up

Work on this activity with a partner or group of classmates. On a large piece of paper, copy the character wheel below. Then complete circles 6–10 with information from the second half of the story.

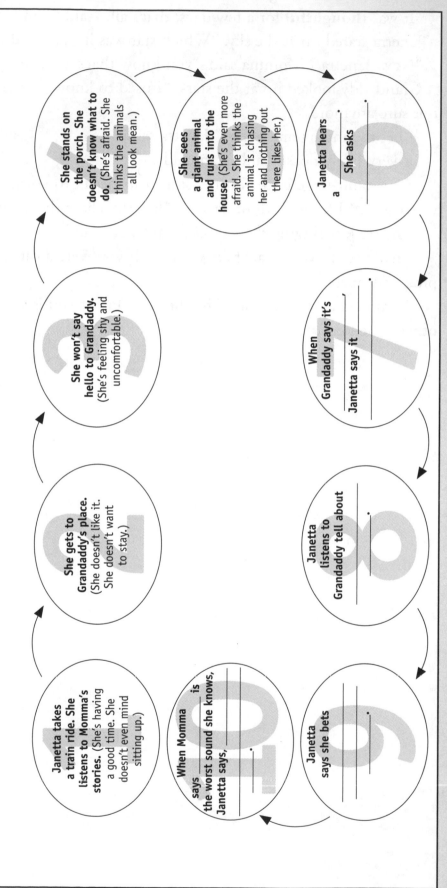

✓Personal Checklist

Read each question and put a check (✓) in the correct box.

1. How well were you able to use what you wrote in Building Background to understand how Janetta felt in this story?
   ☐ 3 (extremely well)
   ☐ 2 (fairly well)
   ☐ 1 (not well)

2. How well were you able to predict how the words *scared, shy, surprised,* and *thoughtful* might be used in this story?
   ☐ 3 (extremely well)
   ☐ 2 (fairly well)
   ☐ 1 (not well)

3. How well were you able to draw conclusions about Janetta's changing feelings?
   ☐ 3 (extremely well)
   ☐ 2 (fairly well)
   ☐ 1 (not well)

4. How well do you understand why Grandaddy tells Janetta about the star?
   ☐ 3 (extremely well)
   ☐ 2 (fairly well)
   ☐ 1 (not well)

5. How well do you understand why Janetta tells her mother, "If you were a cat, you'd be tapping your feet"?
   ☐ 3 (extremely well)
   ☐ 2 (fairly well)
   ☐ 1 (not well)

Vocabulary Check

Look back at the work you did in the Vocabulary Builder. Then answer each question by circling the correct letter.

1. When Grandaddy says that the mule was "thoughtful for a few days," what did he mean?
   a. The mule did nice things for others for a few days.
   b. The mule thought about things deeply for a few days.
   c. The mule was extra careful for a few days.

2. Which word means the opposite of *scared*?
   a. unafraid
   b. frightened
   c. fearful

3. What would a shy person be most likely to do?
   a. introduce himself or herself to a stranger
   b. sing a song in front of a crowd
   c. sit quietly by himself or herself in a corner

4. Which word means the same thing as *surprised*?
   a. bored
   b. startled
   c. ashamed

5. Which word describes someone who sleeps with a light on all night?
   a. thoughtful
   b. shy
   c. scared

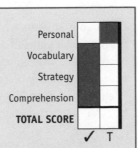

Add the numbers that you just checked to get your Personal Checklist score. Fill in your score here. Then turn to page 203 and transfer your score onto Graph 1.

Personal
Vocabulary
Strategy
Comprehension
TOTAL SCORE
✓ T

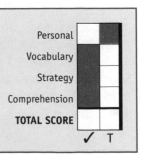

Check your answers with your teacher. Give yourself 1 point for each correct answer, and fill in your Vocabulary score here. Then turn to page 203 and transfer your score onto Graph 1.

Personal
Vocabulary
Strategy
Comprehension
TOTAL SCORE
✓ T

Strategy Check

Review the story and the character wheel that you made in the Strategy Follow-up. Then answer these questions:

1. When Janetta hears the hoot owl, why do you think she thinks it is "a terrible sound"?

    a. The sound hurts her ears.

    b. She is in an angry mood.

    c. She is scared by the sound.

2. Why do you think Janetta is so interested in Grandaddy's story about the star?

    a. She wants to know if the star hurt itself.

    b. The star felt the same as Janetta when it got here.

    c. She wants to know if she can talk to the star.

3. Why do you think Janetta asks if the star was scared when it saw the mule?

    a. She figures a star has never seen a mule before and might be scared.

    b. She was remembering how she felt when she first saw the mule.

    c. Both of the above answers are correct.

4. What does Janetta say to show that she is changing her mind about the mule?

    a. She asks if the mule chased the star the way it chased her.

    b. She bets the mule remembers which star fell to Earth.

    c. She says, "If you were a mule, you'd be tapping your feet."

5. Why does Janetta tell her mother, "If you were a cat, you'd be tapping your feet"?

    a. She's starting to be unafraid and to think more like Grandaddy.

    b. She is making fun of Grandaddy.

    c. She's too afraid to chase the cats away.

Comprehension Check

Review the story if necessary. Then answer these questions:

1. Why is Momma bringing Janetta to Grandaddy's?

    a. She wants to take a train ride.

    b. Grandaddy wants help on the farm.

    c. She wants Janetta to meet Grandaddy.

2. Why do you think Janetta thinks the animals are mean-looking?

    a. The animals keep giving her mean and nasty looks.

    b. She's never seen animals like them and thinks they're mean.

    c. She's seen animals just like them and knows they're mean.

3. What starts to make Janetta change her mind about the farm?

    a. Grandaddy's cat

    b. Grandaddy's story

    c. Grandaddy's mule

4. Why does Grandaddy tell the story of the star?

    a. He's trying to make Janetta feel better.

    b. He's trying to make Janetta more afraid.

    c. He's trying to make Janetta's Momma angry.

5. At the end of the story, why does Momma say, "One of you is as bad as the other"?

    a. She thinks it's bad that they are both telling lies.

    b. She thinks they're both beginning to think alike.

    c. She thinks they're both trying to make her angry.

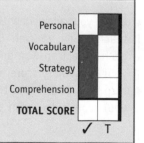

Check your answers with your teacher. Give yourself 1 point for each correct answer, and fill in your Strategy score here. Then turn to page 203 and transfer your score onto Graph 1.

Personal
Vocabulary
Strategy
Comprehension
TOTAL SCORE
✓ T

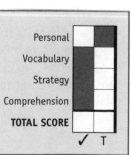

Check your answers with your teacher. Give yourself 1 point for each correct answer, and fill in your Comprehension score here. Then turn to page 203 and transfer your score onto Graph 1.

Personal
Vocabulary
Strategy
Comprehension
TOTAL SCORE
✓ T

Extending

Choose one or both of these activities:

DRAW OR BUILD GRANDADDY'S PLACE

Using the descriptions that the author provides, draw a picture or build a diorama of Grandaddy's place. Look back at the story and try to include as many details as possible. For example, the story mentions cats, chickens, a mule, and a hoot owl. It also mentions that the house has a porch and a fence around it. Share your picture or diorama with your classmates. Point out and explain some of the details you've included.

WRITE ABOUT *YOUR* GRANDPARENTS' PLACE

Write a story about a visit to your grandparents' place. You can write a true story, or you can make one up. Include as many details about where they live as possible. Also tell what you do and how you feel when you go to visit them.

Resources

Books

Griffith, Helen V. *Grandaddy and Janetta*. Greenwillow Books, 1993.

———. *Grandaddy's Place*. Greenwillow Books, 1987.

———. *Grandaddy's Stars*. Greenwillow Books, 1995.

chattered

fast

flew

ground

noticed

seen

sky

slow

soared

sunrise

sunset

talked

Ostriches, or The Birds Nobody Noticed

Building Background

The selection you are about to read is a modern story that is written in the style of a traditional tale. **Traditional tales** include legends, tall tales, folktales, and myths.

In **folktales**, the characters are often animals that act like people. Their personalities are usually "flat," or one-sided. For example, a character might be clever and hard-working or foolish and lazy.

Myths are traditional tales that usually explain certain things in nature. For example, a myth might explain why there are solar eclipses or why elephants have trunks.

On your own or with a partner, recall some of the traditional tales that you have read or heard. Who were the characters in these tales? What were their personalities like? What, if anything, did the tales explain?

Vocabulary Builder

1. Study the vocabulary words in the margin. Each word is half of a pair of antonyms (words with opposite meanings) or synonyms (words with the same meaning).

2. Write the antonym pairs on Clipboard #1.

3. Write the synonym pairs on Clipboard #2.

4. As you read this story, underline any other antonym or synonym pairs that you find.

5. Save your work. You will use it again in the Vocabulary Check.

CLIPBOARD 1

Antonym Pairs (opposites)

1. _____

2. _____

3. _____

CLIPBOARD 2

Synonym Pairs (same meanings)

1. _____

2. _____

3. _____

Strategy Builder

Identifying Causes and Effects in Stories

- Many stories contain cause-and-effect relationships. A **cause** tells *why* something happened. An **effect** tells *what* happened.

- To find a cause-and-effect relationship while you read, ask yourself, "What happened?" and "Why did it happen?" Doing this will help you understand what has happened in the story so far. It also will help you predict what might happen next.

- As you read the following paragraph, think about what happens, and why.

> Joey was really hungry, so he made himself a big turkey sandwich. Just as Joey was about to eat, his dog Sly walked up and gave Joey his paw. Joey broke off a corner of his sandwich and gave it to Sly. Sly gobbled the sandwich and rolled over twice. Joey gave Sly another piece of his sandwich. Sly gobbled it up and howled as if he were singing. Joey gave Sly another piece of his sandwich. Suddenly Joey realized he had given Sly all of his sandwich! Joey got up and made another sandwich.

- If you wanted to track the causes and effects in this paragraph, you could put them on a **cause-and-effect chain**. It might look like this:

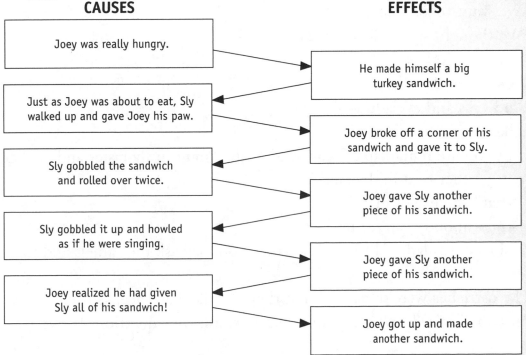

CAUSES

- Joey was really hungry.
- Just as Joey was about to eat, Sly walked up and gave Joey his paw.
- Sly gobbled the sandwich and rolled over twice.
- Sly gobbled it up and howled as if he were singing.
- Joey realized he had given Sly all of his sandwich!

EFFECTS

- He made himself a big turkey sandwich.
- Joey broke off a corner of his sandwich and gave it to Sly.
- Joey gave Sly another piece of his sandwich.
- Joey gave Sly another piece of his sandwich.
- Joey got up and made another sandwich.

Ostriches, or The Birds Nobody Noticed

by Angela Mackworth-Young

As you read the first part of this story, you can apply the strategies that you just learned. To find the causes and effects, keep asking yourself, "What happened?" and "Why did it happen?"

There was a time, a long time ago, when ostriches could fly. They lived in the heart of the heart of Africa and they **flew** faster and farther than any other bird in the land. But they were small, unremarkable birds: when they were in the **sky**, no one could see them, and when they were on the **ground**, everyone ignored them.

The one thing in the world the ostriches wanted was to be **seen**, to be **noticed**. So they flew as **fast** and as far as only they could to find Zushkaali, who was the wise man of those times.

Zushkaali was sitting cross-legged on the dry red ground. He wore his multicolored turban and his multicolored robe, and he wasn't surprised to see the ostriches. He had been expecting them.

The ostriches all **talked** at the same time. They always did.

"We want to be spectacularly shaped—"

"Definitely different—"

"Remarkable, noticeable—"

"We want to be seen."

"We thought we could ask the camels—"

"And the giraffes—"

"For legs and necks—"

"And eyes and eyelashes—"

"Like theirs."

"But you are remarkable," said Zushkaali. "You can fly faster and farther than any other bird in the land."

"What's the use of that—"

"When nobody can see us?"

Zushkaali smiled. "All right," he said, "you may ask the camels and the giraffes—"

The ostriches were so excited that they all talked at once, as usual.

Zushkaali raised his voice. "But you must ask your questions between

sunrise and **sunset** on the same day. And you must be sure to ask the eagle for wings like his—"

But the ostriches were already gone.

The ostriches flew like the wind over the red desert. They found the camels resting in a shady oasis and they swooped down, skidding to a halt and sending flurries of sand up the camels' noses.

"We've come to ask—"

"Could we have—"

"Legs like yours—"

"Please?"

The head camel snorted, opened one eye, and moved his jaw slowly from side to side, the way camels do.

"We never," he said in his deep, **slow** voice, "ever . . . discuss anything . . . until the sun is low in the sky. Far too hot." The camel closed his eye.

The ostriches **chattered** and skittered about, trying to persuade the camels to talk, but they would not.

As the day was drawing to a close, the head camel at last stood up, back legs first the way camels do, and shuffled off to talk to the other camels. The ostriches looked longingly at his legs.

When the head camel returned, he said, "You may all have legs like ours . . . but only two. Four would look silly on a bird."

The ostriches **soared** into the sky, screeching their thanks so loudly that they didn't hear the head camel say, "And we suggest you ask the eagle for wings like his."

The ostriches found the giraffes grazing the tops of the trees in the green valley. They landed on the giraffes' backs. The sun was red and round and low in the sky.

"We've come to ask—"

"Could we have—"

"Necks and eyes and eyelashes—"

"Like yours—"

"Please?"

"Yes," said the giraffes, who were a kindly sort, "you may."

The ostriches soared into the air just as the red sun set.

"Don't forget you'll need wings like the eagle's," called the giraffes, but the ostriches were already out of sight.

When full darkness came, the ostriches fell from the sky, exhausted but happy, at the foot of a dead tree. They slept exactly where they landed.

Stop here for the Strategy Break.

Strategy Break

If you were to create a cause-and-effect chain for this story so far, it might look like this:

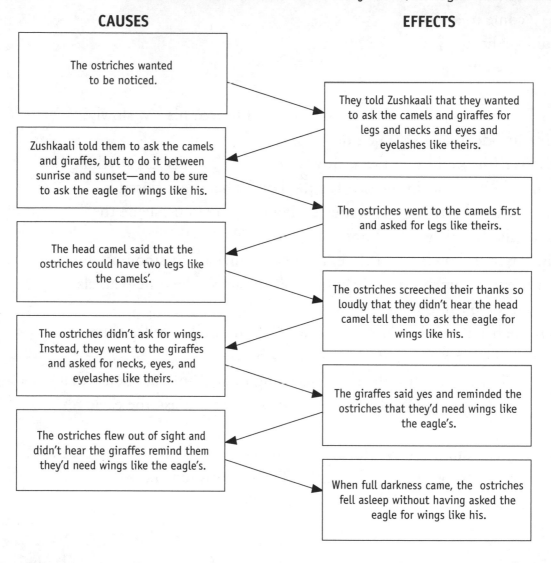

CAUSES	EFFECTS
The ostriches wanted to be noticed.	They told Zushkaali that they wanted to ask the camels and giraffes for legs and necks and eyes and eyelashes like theirs.
Zushkaali told them to ask the camels and giraffes, but to do it between sunrise and sunset—and to be sure to ask the eagle for wings like his.	The ostriches went to the camels first and asked for legs like theirs.
The head camel said that the ostriches could have two legs like the camels'.	The ostriches screeched their thanks so loudly that they didn't hear the head camel tell them to ask the eagle for wings like his.
The ostriches didn't ask for wings. Instead, they went to the giraffes and asked for necks, eyes, and eyelashes like theirs.	The giraffes said yes and reminded the ostriches that they'd need wings like the eagle's.
The ostriches flew out of sight and didn't hear the giraffes remind them they'd need wings like the eagle's.	When full darkness came, the ostriches fell asleep without having asked the eagle for wings like his.

 Go on reading to see what happens.

Zushkaali came to stand beside the dead tree, and the eagle, whose tree it was, spread his mighty wings and floated down onto Zushkaali's shoulder.

The pale moon glowed, and the eagle's eyes filled with tears.

"Couldn't I *give* them wings like mine while they're asleep?" he said.

"No," said Zushkaali, "you know that you cannot. The ostriches must ask before you can give, and time for asking is past."

"But they'll never be able to fly," said the eagle, and his tears splashed down.

The ostriches woke in a tangle of long, long legs and long, long necks. They looked at each other through large, beautiful, long-lashed eyes.

"How spectacularly shaped—"

"How definitely different—"

"How remarkable—"

"How noticeable we are."

The ostriches wobbled on their legs and struggled to hold up their necks, and then they flapped their wings. They ran from side to side to catch the wind. They hopped and they jumped. But whatever they did, they could not take off.

"The eagle," they said, as they slumped to the ground, looking at their hopelessly small wings, "we should have asked the eagle."

The ostriches hung their long necks and dragged their feet across the green valley toward the red desert where they lived. No one spoke. But as they walked, their legs grew stronger and their strides grew longer, and a noise spread across the land. Every single animal the ostriches passed stared and called out. They said that the ostriches were spectacularly shaped and definitely different. They said that they were remarkable, noticeable, tall-striding birds.

By the time the ostriches reached the edge of the red desert, their heads were high and their eyes were shining. They could be *seen*.

The eagle was waiting for them. He stood in a pool of his own tears.

"I wish I could help," he said sadly, "but it's too late."

"It's all right," said one ostrich. "We're spectacularly shaped and definitely different. And that's what we've always wanted."

"I can see that," said the eagle, staring up at the ostrich. "But you can't fly, and that is a terrible thing for a bird."

"When we could fly, no one noticed us," said another ostrich.

"But now," said a third, "they can't help but notice us," and she danced on her long legs in the red sand. "Besides," she added, bending her long neck down to the eagle, "a bird who *can't* fly must be a *truly* remarkable bird. Don't you think?" ●

Strategy Follow-up

Complete this cause-and-effect chain for the second part of the story. Copy it onto another sheet of paper if you need more room to write. Some of the chain has been filled in for you.

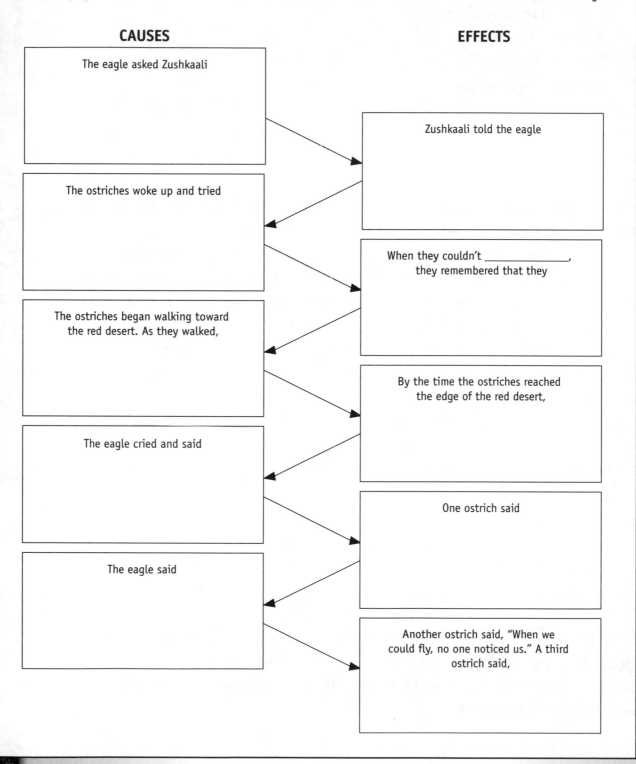

CAUSES

The eagle asked Zushkaali

The ostriches woke up and tried

The ostriches began walking toward the red desert. As they walked,

The eagle cried and said

The eagle said

EFFECTS

Zushkaali told the eagle

When they couldn't _____, they remembered that they

By the time the ostriches reached the edge of the red desert,

One ostrich said

Another ostrich said, "When we could fly, no one noticed us." A third ostrich said,

✓Personal Checklist

Read each question and put a check (✓) in the correct box.

1. How well were you able to use the information in Building Background to help you understand the characters and events in this story?
   - ☐ 3 (extremely well)
   - ☐ 2 (fairly well)
   - ☐ 1 (not well)

2. How well were you able to list synonym pairs and antonym pairs in the Vocabulary Builder?
   - ☐ 3 (extremely well)
   - ☐ 2 (fairly well)
   - ☐ 1 (not well)

3. How well were you able to identify the causes and effects in this story?
   - ☐ 3 (extremely well)
   - ☐ 2 (fairly well)
   - ☐ 1 (not well)

4. How well do you understand why the eagle cries when he sees the sleeping ostriches?
   - ☐ 3 (extremely well)
   - ☐ 2 (fairly well)
   - ☐ 1 (not well)

5. How well do you understand why the ostriches say, "A bird who *can't* fly must be a *truly* remarkable bird"?
   - ☐ 3 (extremely well)
   - ☐ 2 (fairly well)
   - ☐ 1 (not well)

Vocabulary Check

Look back at the work you did in the Vocabulary Builder. Then answer each question by circling the correct letter.

1. Which vocabulary word is a synonym for the word *flew*?
   a. noticed
   b. soared
   c. chattered

2. Which vocabulary word is an antonym of the word *sky*?
   a. ground
   b. sunrise
   c. sunset

3. Which definition best fits the word *chattered*?
   a. talked hardly at all about very important things
   b. talked constantly and slowly about boring things
   c. talked constantly and quickly about silly things

4. Which antonym pair can be used to describe times of day?
   a. sunrise/sunset
   b. ground/sky
   c. fast/slow

5. Which of the following describes what the ostriches want most?
   a. to be noticed
   b. to be seen
   c. both of the above

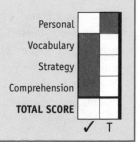

Add the numbers that you just checked to get your Personal Checklist score. Fill in your score here. Then turn to page 203 and transfer your score onto Graph 1.

Personal | Vocabulary | Strategy | Comprehension | **TOTAL SCORE** ✓ T

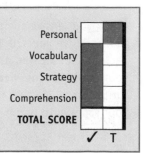

Check your answers with your teacher. Give yourself 1 point for each correct answer, and fill in your Vocabulary score here. Then turn to page 203 and transfer your score onto Graph 1.

Personal | Vocabulary | Strategy | Comprehension | **TOTAL SCORE** ✓ T

Strategy Check

Look back at the cause-and-effect chain that you completed for the second part of this story. Then answer these questions:

1. What was the effect of the eagle's question to Zushkaali?
   a. He said the eagle couldn't give the ostriches wings.
   b. He told the eagle to give the ostriches wings.
   c. He told the eagle to take away the ostriches' wings.

2. What was the effect when the ostriches woke up and tried to fly?
   a. Their new wings were so stiff that they wouldn't work.
   b. They remembered that they hadn't asked the eagle for wings.
   c. They cried and asked the eagle to give them wings like his.

3. What caused all the animals to say that the ostriches were remarkable?
   a. As they walked, their strides grew longer.
   b. Their wings grew stronger and they flew.
   c. They hung their necks and dragged their feet.

4. What effect did being called remarkable have?
   a. It made the ostriches sad and discouraged.
   b. It made the ostriches shy and embarrassed.
   c. It made the ostriches proud and happy.

5. What caused one ostrich to say that a bird who can't fly must be a truly remarkable bird?
   a. The eagle said that the ostriches were spectacular and different.
   b. The eagle said that he could still give the ostriches wings like his.
   c. The eagle said that not being able to fly is a terrible thing for a bird.

Comprehension Check

Review the story if necessary. Then answer these questions:

1. What do the ostriches ask for from the giraffes?
   a. necks, eyes, and eyelashes like theirs
   b. long, thin legs like theirs
   c. huge, strong wings like theirs

2. Why do Zushkaali, the camels, and the giraffes tell the ostriches to ask the eagle for wings like his?
   a. They are jealous and want to make the ostriches unhappy.
   b. They want the ostriches to be unremarkable and unnoticeable.
   c. They know the ostriches won't be able to fly without them.

3. Why won't Zushkaali let the eagle give the ostriches wings like his?
   a. The ostriches won't be happy with eagle wings.
   b. The ostriches still have time to ask for them.
   c. The ostriches didn't ask for them in time.

4. Which words best describe the ostriches in this story?
   a. clever and thoughtful
   b. careless and forgetful
   c. fearful and shy

5. What do you think this tale is trying to explain?
   a. why ostriches can't fly
   b. why ostriches are silly
   c. why ostriches have wings

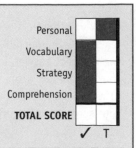

Check your answers with your teacher. Give yourself 1 point for each correct answer, and fill in your Strategy score here. Then turn to page 203 and transfer your score onto Graph 1.

Personal
Vocabulary
Strategy
Comprehension
TOTAL SCORE
✓ T

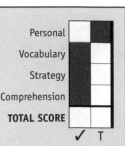

Check your answers with your teacher. Give yourself 1 point for each correct answer, and fill in your Comprehension score here. Then turn to page 203 and transfer your score onto Graph 1.

Personal
Vocabulary
Strategy
Comprehension
TOTAL SCORE
✓ T

Extending

Choose one or both of these activities:

WRITE ABOUT OSTRICHES

Find out more about ostriches by digging into the Internet or your school or local library. Find out such information as what ostriches eat, where they live, how long they live, and how large full-grown ostriches can get. Present your findings in a written report. Illustrate your report with copies of photographs or with pictures that you draw yourself.

TELL A TRADITIONAL TALE

Traditional tales were originally shared orally, rather than written down. Find a traditional tale and share it orally with your class, a small group, or a younger class. You might work with other students to create a puppet play, a skit, or a dramatic reading to share your tale.

Resources

Books

Aardema, Verna. *How the Ostrich Got Its Long Neck: A Tale from the Akamba of Kenya.* Scholastic, 1995.

————. *The Lonely Lioness and the Ostrich Chicks: A Masai Tale.* Knopf, 1996.

Baumgartner, Barbara. *Crocodile! Crocodile!* Stories Told Round the World. Dorling Kindersley, 1994.

Bryan, Ashley. *Lion and the Ostrich Chicks and Other African Folk Tales.* Aladdin Paperbacks, 1996.

King-Smith, Dick. *Cuckoo Child.* Hyperion Press, 1999.

Switzer, Merebeth. *Ostrich.* Nature's Children. Grolier Educational Corporation, 1994.

Web Site

http://www.teachervision.fen.com
Search for "African folk tales." This site gives examples of various types of African folk tales.

What Makes a Bird a Bird?

Building Background

The selection you are about to read names several different birds. How many birds can you name? By yourself or with a partner, make a list of as many birds as you can. Then, as you read this selection, add to your list the names of any other birds that you find.

Do you know what makes a bird a bird? If you do, terrific! If you don't, read your list of birds again and think about what they all have in common. Next to your list, write what you think might make a bird a bird. Then read this selection to find the answer.

Vocabulary Builder

call

camouflaged

chicks

molt

nest

preen

1. Sometimes when you read nonfiction, you come across words that are related to a particular topic. Those words are called **specialized vocabulary.** When you read "Laughter Is Good Medicine," for example, some of the specialized vocabulary included the words *cure, disease, germs, immune system,* and *blood pressure.* All of these words are related to health in some way.
2. Look at the words below. The words in Column 1 are specialized vocabulary from "What Makes a Bird a Bird?"
3. Draw a line from each word in Column 1 to its definition in Column 2. Then think about how each word might be used in a selection about birds.

COLUMN 1	COLUMN 2
call	baby birds
nest	soften and straighten
preen	shed or lose
camouflaged	place for laying eggs
molt	sing or talk
chicks	disguised

4. Save your work. You will use it again in the Vocabulary Check.

Strategy Builder

Comparing and Contrasting While You Read

- Authors often compare and contrast things when they write. **Comparing** means telling how two or more things are alike. **Contrasting** means telling how two or more things are different. In Lesson 4 the author of "Dogs Who 'Think'" compares and contrasts German shepherds, poodles, and dachshunds by telling how they are alike and different.

- Think back to the story "Ostriches, or The Birds Nobody Noticed." Some of the characters in the story are ostriches, camels, giraffes, and an eagle. If you wanted to show how these creatures are alike and different, you could create a **features chart** like this:

Features Chart for "Ostriches, or The Birds Nobody Noticed"

	long legs	long neck	wings
ostriches	yes	yes	yes
camels	yes	yes	no
giraffes	yes	yes	no
eagle	no	no	yes

What Makes a Bird a Bird?

by May Garelick

As you read this selection, apply the strategies that you just learned. Look for how the author compares and contrasts birds with the other creatures mentioned.

In trees and in bushes, at the edge of a brook, on the ground, and in the air, birds are flying, singing, calling, bathing, nesting.

How do we know that a bird is a bird? What makes it a bird?

Is it a bird because it flies?

A fly flies. So do butterflies, ladybugs, dragonflies, and bees. But these are not birds. They are insects.

Many insects fly. Not as fast as birds, not as far as birds, but many insects fly.

A bat flies, too, but it is not a bird. All day bats hang upside down, asleep in hollow trees or in caves. At night they fly, catching insects to eat as they fly around.

Bats fly, insects fly, birds fly, and other things fly, too.

Did you know that there is even a fish that flies? Like all fish, a flying fish lives most of the time in water. But if an enemy comes near, it can jump up out of the water, dart through the air, and escape.

Flying fish don't fly high and they don't fly far, but they fly higher and farther than some *birds.*

If there are flying insects, flying bats, and even flying fish, then it's not flying that makes a bird a bird.

As a matter of fact, you know a *bird* that doesn't fly.

Have you ever seen a chicken fly? Hardly ever. Sometimes a chicken tries to fly. But it doesn't get far. To get anywhere a chicken walks.

Is a chicken a bird? Yes.

Another bird that doesn't fly is the ostrich.

It's the biggest bird in the world, but it can't fly. An ostrich can run fast, though—even faster than a horse. No wonder. It has very long legs. That's why the ostrich is such a fast runner.

Can you think of another bird that can't fly?

A penguin can't fly. Penguins walk. Down to the water they waddle, and into the sea for a swim.

If the ostrich can't fly, and penguins and chickens can't fly, what makes them birds?

Are they birds because they have wings?

Birds have wings, all right. But look at a fly flying around. You can see its wings. And dragonflies and butterflies and bees have wings, too.

Not all insects have wings, but those that fly have to have wings.

Then what about a chicken and an ostrich? They have wings, but do not fly. Why? Their wings are too small to lift their bodies up in the air.

The penguin's little wings are like flippers. They're fine for swimming, but too small to lift the penguin up into the air.

Still an ostrich, a chicken, and a penguin are birds. So it isn't wings that make a bird a bird.

 Stop here for the Strategy Break.

Strategy Break

If you were to make a features chart for this selection so far, it might look like this:

Features Chart for Part 1 of "What Makes a Bird a Bird?"

	can fly	have wings
MOST BIRDS	yes	yes
flies	yes	yes
butterflies	yes	yes
ladybugs	yes	yes
dragonflies	yes	yes
bees	yes	yes
bats	yes	yes
flying fish	yes	no
chickens	no	yes
ostriches	no	yes
penguins	no	yes

As you continue reading, keep looking for the ways that birds and other creatures are alike and different.

Go on reading.

Is a bird a thing that sings?

Birds sing and **call** to each other, especially in the spring. Some birds sing, some birds call, some cluck, some quack. That's how birds talk to each other.

One bird's song many mean, "This is my tree. Keep away." Usually other birds do keep away. If they don't, there's a fight.

"Chiree, chiree," a bird sings to a lady bird. Maybe his song means, "Come join me."

A mother hen clucks to her **chicks** to tell them that food is here.

"Cluck, cluck." And her baby chicks come running.

A duck quacks to her ducklings.

"Quack, quack." And her ducklings follow her.

"Peep, peep," call the baby robins. And their parents know that the babies are hungry.

Birds sing and call messages to each other. But singing and calling is not what makes a bird a bird.

Lots of *insects* sing and call their messages to each other, too.

Crickets chirp, and grasshoppers hum. Katydids repeat their rhythmic song all night long. *Katydid, katydid, katy didn't.* And of all the insects, the tree cricket's song at night is the most beautiful. But these singers and callers are not birds. So it isn't singing that makes a bird a bird.

Then what *is* the special thing that makes a bird a bird?

Is it a bird if it builds a **nest?**

Birds build nests in trees, in bushes, under eaves, in barns. Sometimes they even build nests in mailboxes—wherever their eggs and their babies will be safe.

Birds' eggs must be kept warm in order to hatch. The nest and the mother's body keep the eggs warm.

But some birds build no nests at all. A whippoorwill lays her eggs on the ground. But the eggs are the color of the ground around them—**camouflaged**—so they are safe.

The penguin that lives in the cold, icy Antarctic builds no nest. The mother lays one egg. Then the father penguin carries the egg on top of his feet, close to his body. That's how he keeps the egg warm for two months, until it is ready to hatch.

Other creatures make nests. Ants and bees, snakes and fish, and rabbits and mice make nests.

Nest building is not the special thing that makes a bird a bird.

Neither is egg laying. All birds lay eggs, it's true. But so do frogs, snakes, fish, bees, mosquitoes, and many other creatures.

So—

It's not flying that makes a bird different from anything else alive.

And it's not having wings.

And it's not singing or calling.

And it's not building nests or laying eggs.

What is it, then, that makes a bird a bird?

Birds have something that no other living thing has. What is it?

FEATHERS!

Only birds have feathers. That's the special thing that makes a bird a bird. A bird has to have feathers to be a bird.

If it flies or not, if it sings or not; anything with feathers is a bird.

Feathers are strong. Try to break or tear one, and you'll see how strong a feather is. Bend a feather so the tip touches the bottom. Watch it spring back. It won't break.

Feathers are light. Hold a feather and you'll see how light it is. You've heard people say that something is "light as a feather."

Feathers are beautiful. They come in all colors. There are red cardinals, blue blue jays, black blackbirds, white doves, green parrots, brown sparrows, and many other colored birds in other colored feathers.

Feathers are useful, too.

They do many things for birds. Their flight feathers make birds the best flyers. Even though other creatures fly, no living creature can fly as long or as far as a bird.

A bird has several layers of feathers. There's a cloak of feathers that helps keep birds warm in winter. Watch a bird on a cold day. It looks like a fat puffball because it has fluffed out its feathers to keep out the cold.

A layer of flat feathers helps keep birds cool in summer. The heat from the bird's body works its way out through these feathers.

Feathers help keep birds dry in the rain. Put a drop of water on a feather, and watch the water slide off.

Birds take good care of their feathers. Some birds bathe in water—ducking, splashing, spreading their wings. Some birds bathe in fine dust. After bathing, they **preen** their feathers carefully with their beaks. From an oil sac at the tail, birds take oil into their beaks to soften and straighten their feathers.

But no matter how well birds clean their feathers, they get brittle and wear out. About once a year birds **molt**—their worn out feathers fall out. Not all at once, just one or two at a time. And as they fall out, new feathers grow in.

You may find some of these old feathers on the ground. Pick them up and look at them.

Feathers are the special things that *make a bird a bird.* ●

Strategy Follow-up

Now fill in this features chart for the second part of "What Makes a Bird a Bird?" Go back and skim the selection for information when you need to.

Features Chart for Part 2 of "What Makes a Bird a Bird?"

	sing and call	build nests	lay eggs	have feathers
MOST BIRDS				
ALL BIRDS				
crickets/tree crickets				
grasshoppers				
katydids				
whippoorwills				
penguins				
ants				
bees				
snakes				
fish				
rabbits				
mice				
frogs				
mosquitoes				

✓Personal Checklist

Read each question and put a check (✓) in the correct box.

1. How well do you understand what makes a bird a bird?
   - ☐ 3 (extremely well)
   - ☐ 2 (fairly well)
   - ☐ 1 (not well)

2. How well do you understand why the words *call, camouflaged, chicks, molt, nest,* and *preen* are specialized vocabulary in this selection?
   - ☐ 3 (extremely well)
   - ☐ 2 (fairly well)
   - ☐ 1 (not well)

3. How well were you able to compare and contrast birds and other creatures?
   - ☐ 3 (extremely well)
   - ☐ 2 (fairly well)
   - ☐ 1 (not well)

4. How well do you understand why not all creatures with wings are birds?
   - ☐ 3 (extremely well)
   - ☐ 2 (fairly well)
   - ☐ 1 (not well)

5. How well do you understand why not all birds fly?
   - ☐ 3 (extremely well)
   - ☐ 2 (fairly well)
   - ☐ 1 (not well)

Vocabulary Check

Look back at the work you did in the Vocabulary Builder. Then answer each question by circling the correct letter.

1. To what topic is the specialized vocabulary in this selection related?
   a. wings
   b. birds
   c. feathers

2. How are a whippoorwill's eggs camouflaged?
   a. They are hidden high in the branches of a tree.
   b. They are the color of the ground around them.
   c. They are the same color as the nest they sit in.

3. What do birds do when they preen their feathers?
   a. They bathe them in water.
   b. They bathe them in fine dust.
   c. They straighten them with oil.

4. What happens when birds molt?
   a. Their feathers fall out.
   b. They clean their feathers.
   c. They build new nests.

5. Which is *not* a way that birds call to each other?
   a. quack
   b. bark
   c. peep

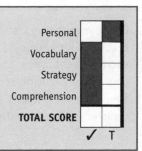

Add the numbers that you just checked to get your Personal Checklist score. Fill in your score here. Then turn to page 203 and transfer your score onto Graph 1.

Personal
Vocabulary
Strategy
Comprehension
TOTAL SCORE
✓ T

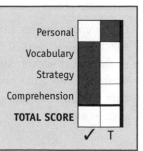

Check your answers with your teacher. Give yourself 1 point for each correct answer, and fill in your Vocabulary score here. Then turn to page 203 and transfer your score onto Graph 1.

Personal
Vocabulary
Strategy
Comprehension
TOTAL SCORE
✓ T

Strategy Check

Look back at the features charts for both parts of this selection. Use them to answer these questions:

1. What do penguins and ostriches have in common?
   a. Neither one has wings.
   b. They both can fly.
   c. Neither one can fly.

2. How are birds and flying fish different?
   a. Only birds have wings.
   b. Only birds can fly.
   c. Only flying fish can fly.

3. Which creature does not build a nest?
   a. fish
   b. snake
   c. whippoorwill

4. What is one thing that all birds do?
   a. build nests
   b. lay eggs
   c. fly

5. How are birds different from all other creatures?
   a. They sing and call.
   b. They have feathers.
   c. They make nests.

Comprehension Check

Review the selection if necessary. Then answer these questions:

1. Which creature can easily fly?
   a. a chicken
   b. an ostrich
   c. a bat

2. How does a father penguin keep an egg warm?
   a. He carries it on top of his feet.
   b. He carries it under his chin.
   c. He carries it under a wing.

3. How do birds send messages?
   a. They flap their wings.
   b. They sing and call.
   c. They preen their feathers.

4. What do all birds look for when they build a nest?
   a. a place that's safe and warm
   b. a place that's cool and damp
   c. a place that's in a tree

5. What is special about feathers?
   a. They are strong, brittle, breakable, and warm.
   b. They are strong, light, beautiful, and useful.
   c. They are dry, dusty, straight, and brittle.

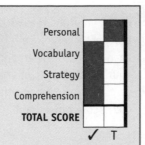

Check your answers with your teacher. Give yourself 1 point for each correct answer, and fill in your Strategy score here. Then turn to page 203 and transfer your score onto Graph 1.

Personal
Vocabulary
Strategy
Comprehension
TOTAL SCORE
✓ T

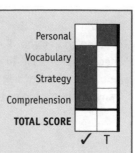

Check your answers with your teacher. Give yourself 1 point for each correct answer, and fill in your Comprehension score here. Then turn to page 203 and transfer your score onto Graph 1.

Personal
Vocabulary
Strategy
Comprehension
TOTAL SCORE
✓ T

Extending

Choose one or more of these activities:

COMPARE AND CONTRAST TWO CREATURES

Choose two creatures that you are interested in learning more about. Using the resources on this page or others, find out as much as you can about the creatures. Then compare and contrast the creatures on a features chart like the ones in this lesson. Next use your chart to write three paragraphs. The first paragraph should tell which creatures you are comparing and contrasting. It also should tell why you chose them. The second paragraph should tell how the creatures are alike. The third paragraph should tell how they are different.

COMPARE BIRDCALLS

Listen to a tape of birdcalls. Choose a few of the calls and write descriptions of how they sound or what they remind you of. Can someone else read your descriptions and mimic, or copy, the calls? Try out your descriptions on friends or family members. Then compare their calls to the ones on the tape.

Resources

Books

Boring, Mel, and Linda Garrow. *Birds, Nests, and Eggs.* Creative Publishing International, 1998.

Burnie, David. *Bird.* Eyewitness Books. Dorling Kindersley, 2000.

Griffin, Steven A., and Elizabeth May Griffin. *Bird Watching for Kids: A Family Bird Watching Guide.* NorthWord Press, 1995.

Harrison, George H. *Backyard Bird Watching for Kids: How to Attract, Feed, and Provide Homes for Birds.* Willow Creek Press, 1997.

Johnson, Jinny. *Children's Guide to Birds.* Simon & Schuster, 1996.

Rupp, Rebecca. *Everything You Never Learned About Birds: Lore and Legends, Science and Nature, Hands-On Projects.* Storey Books, 1995.

Williams, Nick. *How Birds Fly.* Nature's Mysteries. Benchmark Books, 1997.

Web Sites

http://www.birds.cornell.edu
This site provides facts, articles, and videos about birds and tells how to protect birds and their habitats.

http://www.pbs.org
Search for "birds." This site allows you to choose links to PBS TV programs about birds.

Audio Recordings

Songs and Sounds of the Canadian Rockies. Neville Recording, 1997.

Stokes Field Guide to Bird Songs: Eastern Region. Time Warner Audio Books, 1997. (Includes 3 compact discs and 64-page booklet)

Videos/DVDs

Audubon Society's Videoguide to Birds of North America 5. Mastervision, 1988.

Birds. Anchor Bay Entertainment, 1995.

Birds and Flying Creatures 1. TMW/Media Group, 1997.

Tell Me Why: Birds and Rodents. Vision Quest Video, 1990.

Petronella (Part 1)

Building Background

The story you are about to read is a fairy tale. **Fairy tales** are make-believe stories with at least one of the following elements, or parts:

- **imaginary characters**, such as wizards, elves, fairies, or dragons

- **imaginary objects**, such as talking trees or magic flutes

- **imaginary settings**, such as magic kingdoms or other planets

- **imaginary events**, such as people disappearing or turning themselves into animals

Many times fairy tales also contain **elements of three**. The number three might be found in the title of a tale, as in "The Three Bears." Or it can be found in the number of important characters, events, or items in a tale.

By yourself or with a partner, brainstorm some tales that contain elements of three. List them on a separate sheet of paper.

Vocabulary Builder

divided

enchanter

fortunes

haughtily

reasonable

rescued

1. The boldfaced words in the following questions can be found in Part 1 of "Petronella." Before you read the tale, answer the questions by yourself or with a partner.
   a. One of the characters in "Petronella" is an **enchanter**. What might an enchanter do in a fairy tale?
   b. Three of the characters in "Petronella" leave home to seek their **fortunes**. What might a fortune be to a character in a fairy tale?
   c. One of the characters in this tale is going to be **rescued**. Who is usually rescued in other fairy tales that you have read? How are they usually rescued?
   d. One of the characters in this tale is a princess who is told to be **reasonable**. What might be reasonable behavior be for a fairy-tale princess?
   e. One of the princes in this tale speaks **haughtily**. Using a haughty voice, say something that a fairy-tale prince might say.

f. In this tale, you will read about a road **divided**. Decide what this road might look like and sketch it on this page.

2. Save your work. You will use it again in the Vocabulary Check.

Strategy Builder

Mapping the Elements of a Story

- One of the main elements of every story is its plot. The **plot** is the sequence of events in a story. In most stories the plot revolves around a problem that the main character or characters have and the steps they take to solve it. For example, in "The Hole in the Road," the plot revolves around the problem of the hole and the steps that the mayor and the townspeople take to try to solve the problem.

- Sometimes a story has a rather complicated plot. In such a case it is helpful to map out the elements of the story on a story map. A **story map** helps you keep track of a story's setting, its characters, the problems, and the solution. A story map also helps you retell the story to someone else.

- Think about the popular fairy tale "Rumpelstiltskin." If you were to create a story map for the tale, it might look like the one below. (Notice the elements of three.)

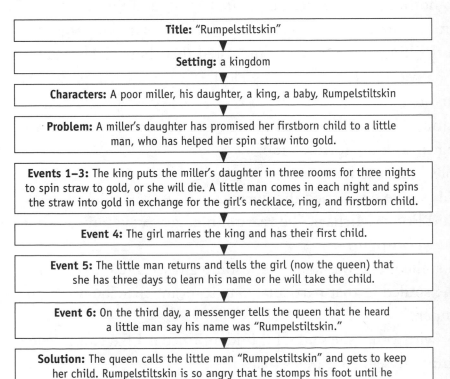

Title: "Rumpelstiltskin"

Setting: a kingdom

Characters: A poor miller, his daughter, a king, a baby, Rumpelstiltskin

Problem: A miller's daughter has promised her firstborn child to a little man, who has helped her spin straw into gold.

Events 1–3: The king puts the miller's daughter in three rooms for three nights to spin straw to gold, or she will die. A little man comes in each night and spins the straw into gold in exchange for the girl's necklace, ring, and firstborn child.

Event 4: The girl marries the king and has their first child.

Event 5: The little man returns and tells the girl (now the queen) that she has three days to learn his name or he will take the child.

Event 6: On the third day, a messenger tells the queen that he heard a little man say his name was "Rumpelstiltskin."

Solution: The queen calls the little man "Rumpelstiltskin" and gets to keep her child. Rumpelstiltskin is so angry that he stomps his foot until he disappears into the ground.

Petronella (Part 1)

by Jay Williams

As you read, apply the strategies that you just learned. In the Strategy Follow-up, you will complete a story map for this part of "Petronella." Also, look for any elements of three and add them to the list you began in Building Background.

In the kingdom of Skyclear Mountain, three princes were always born to the king and queen. The oldest prince was always called Michael, the middle prince was always called George, and the youngest was always called Peter. When they were grown, they always went out to seek their **fortunes**. What happened to the oldest prince and the middle prince no one ever knew. But the youngest prince always **rescued** a princess, brought her home, and in time ruled over the kingdom. That was the way it had always been. And so far as anyone knew, that was the way it would always be.

Until now.

Now was the time of King Peter the twenty-sixth and Queen Blossom. An oldest prince was born, and a middle prince. But the youngest prince turned out to be a girl.

"Well," said the king gloomily, "we can't call her Peter. We'll have to call her Petronella. And what's to be done about it, I'm sure I don't know."

There was nothing to be done. The years passed, and the time came for the princes to go out and seek their fortunes. Michael and George said good-bye to the king and queen and mounted their horses. Then out came Petronella. She was dressed in traveling clothes, with her bag packed and a sword by her side.

"If you think," she said, "that I'm going to sit at home, you are mistaken. I'm going to seek my fortune, too."

"Impossible!" said the king.

"What will people say?" cried the queen.

"Look," said Prince Michael, "be **reasonable**, Pet. Stay home. Sooner or later a prince will turn up here."

Petronella smiled. She was a tall, handsome girl with flaming red hair and when she smiled in that particular way it meant that she was trying to keep her temper.

"I'm going with you," she said. "I'll find a prince if I have to rescue one from something myself. And that's that."

The grooms brought out her horse, she said good-bye to her parents, and away she went behind her two brothers.

They traveled into the flatlands below Skyclear Mountain. After many days, they entered a great dark forest. They came to a place where the road **divided** into three, and there at the fork sat a little, wrinkled old man covered with dust and spiderwebs.

Prince Michael said **haughtily**, "Where do these roads go, old man?"

"The road on the right goes to the city of Gratz," the man replied. "The road in the center goes to the castle of Blitz. The road on the left goes to the house of Albion the **enchanter**. And that's one."

"What do you mean by 'And that's one'?" asked Prince George.

"I mean," said the old man, "that I am forced to sit on this spot without stirring, and that I must answer one question from each person who passes by. And that's two."

Petronella's kind heart was touched. "Is there anything I can do to help you?" she asked.

The old man sprang to his feet. The dust fell from him in clouds.

"You have already done so," he said. "For that question is the one which releases me. I have sat here for sixty-two years waiting for someone to ask me that." He snapped his fingers with joy. "In return, I will tell you anything you wish to know."

"Where can I find a prince?" Petronella said promptly.

"There is one in the house of Albion the enchanter," the old man answered.

"Ah," said Petronella, "then that is where I am going."

"In that case I will leave you," said her oldest brother. "For I am going to the castle of Blitz to see if I can find my fortune there."

"Good luck," said Prince George. "For I am going to the city of Gratz. I have a feeling my fortune is there."

They embraced her and rode away.

Petronella looked thoughtfully at the old man, who was combing spiderwebs and dust out of his beard. "May I ask you something else?" she said.

"Of course. Anything."

"Suppose I wanted to rescue that prince from the enchanter. How would I go about it? I haven't any experience in such things, you see."

The old man chewed a piece of his beard. "I do not know everything," he said, after a moment. "I know that there are three magical secrets which, if you can get them from him, will help you."

"How can I get them?" asked Petronella.

"Offer to work for him. He will set you three tasks, and if you can do them you may demand a reward for each. You must ask him for a comb for your hair, a mirror to look into, and a ring for your finger."

"And then?"

"I do not know. I only know that when you rescue the prince, you can use these things to escape from the enchanter."

"It doesn't sound easy," sighed Petronella.

"Nothing we really want is easy," said the old man. "Look at me—I have wanted my freedom, and I've had to wait sixty-two years for it."

Petronella said good-bye to him. She mounted her horse and galloped along the third road.

It ended at a low, rambling house with a red roof. It was a comfortable-looking house, surrounded by gardens and stables and trees heavy with fruit.

 Stop here for the Strategy Break.

Strategy Break

If you were to stop and create a story map for "Petronella" so far, it might look like this:

Title: "Petronella" (Part 1)

▼

Setting: the kingdom of Skyclear Mountain

▼

Characters: King Peter, Queen Blossom, Prince Michael, Prince George, Petronella, old man

▼

Problem: Petronella needs to rescue a prince so she can rule the kingdom.

▼

Event 1: Petronella and her brothers set off to find their fortunes.

▼

Event 2: Petronella and her brothers meet an old man at a road that divides into three.

▼

Event 3: By asking what she can do to help the old man, Petronella sets him free.

▼

Event 4: In return, the old man tells Petronella where she can find a prince. He also explains the three magical secrets, tasks, and rewards that she must know in order to rescue the prince and escape from the enchanter.

To be continued . . .

As you continue reading, keep paying attention to the events in this tale. Also note any elements of three and add them to your list.

Go on reading to see what happens.

On the lawn, in an armchair, sat a handsome young man with his eyes closed and his face turned to the sky.

Petronella tied her horse to the gate and walked across the lawn.

"Is this the house of Albion the enchanter?" she said.

The young man blinked up at her in surprise.

"I think so," he said. "Yes, I'm sure it is."

"And who are you?"

The young man yawned and stretched. "I am Prince Ferdinand of Firebright," he replied. "Would you mind stepping aside? I'm trying to get a suntan and you're standing in the way."

Petronella snorted. "You don't sound like much of a prince," she said.

"That's funny," said the young man, closing his eyes. "That's what my father always says."

At that moment the door of the house opened. Out came a man dressed all in black and silver. He was tall and thin, and his eyes were as black as a cloud full of thunder. Petronella knew at once that he must be the enchanter.

He bowed to her politely. "What can I do for you?"

"I wish to work for you," said Petronella boldly.

Albion nodded. "I cannot refuse you," he said. "But I warn you, it will be dangerous. Tonight I will give you a task. If you do it, I will reward you. If you fail, you must die."

Petronella glanced at the prince and sighed. "If I must, I must," she said. "Very well." ●

Strategy Follow-up

Now continue the story map for Part 1 of "Petronella." (You will read Part 2 in Lesson 10.) Start your map with Event 5. Parts of the events have been filled in for you.

Problem: Petronella needs to rescue a prince so she can rule the kingdom.

▼

Event 5: Petronella meets

Then she meets

▼

Event 6: Petronella asks

▼

Event 7: Albion tells her

▼

Event 8: Petronella says

▼

To be continued . . .

✓Personal Checklist

Read each question and put a check (✓) in the correct box.

1. How well were you able to find the elements of three in this part of "Petronella"?
   - ☐ 3 (extremely well)
   - ☐ 2 (fairly well)
   - ☐ 1 (not well)

2. How well were you able to answer the questions in the Vocabulary Builder?
   - ☐ 3 (extremely well)
   - ☐ 2 (fairly well)
   - ☐ 1 (not well)

3. How well were you able to fill in the events on your story map for this part of the tale?
   - ☐ 3 (extremely well)
   - ☐ 2 (fairly well)
   - ☐ 1 (not well)

4. How well do you understand why Petronella is working for Albion the enchanter?
   - ☐ 3 (extremely well)
   - ☐ 2 (fairly well)
   - ☐ 1 (not well)

5. How well do you understand how Petronella feels about the Prince Ferdinand?
   - ☐ 3 (extremely well)
   - ☐ 2 (fairly well)
   - ☐ 1 (not well)

Vocabulary Check

Look back at the work you did in the Vocabulary Builder. Then answer each question by circling the correct letter.

1. When Petronella wants to seek her fortune, why does Michael tell her to be reasonable?
   a. He doesn't want her to have a fortune of her own.
   b. He doesn't want her to get any of his fortune.
   c. He doesn't think she is acting like a typical princess.

2. When Petronella and her brothers go to seek their fortunes, what are they most likely seeking?
   a. a fortuneteller
   b. money and property
   c. a lucky break

3. What does the divided road look like in this tale?
   a. one road becoming three roads
   b. one road becoming two roads
   c. one road ending suddenly

4. Which sentence is spoken haughtily in this tale?
   a. "Nothing we really want is easy."
   b. "Is there anything I can do to help you?"
   c. "Where do these roads go, old man?"

5. What is another name for an enchanter?
   a. a comedian
   b. a magician
   c. a singer

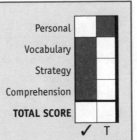

Add the numbers that you just checked to get your Personal Checklist score. Fill in your score here. Then turn to page 203 and transfer your score onto Graph 1.

Personal
Vocabulary
Strategy
Comprehension
TOTAL SCORE
✓ T

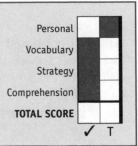

Check your answers with your teacher. Give yourself 1 point for each correct answer, and fill in your Vocabulary score here. Then turn to page 203 and transfer your score onto Graph 1.

Personal
Vocabulary
Strategy
Comprehension
TOTAL SCORE
✓ T

Strategy Check

Look back at your story maps for this lesson. Use them to help you answer these questions:

1. Which event makes it seem most possible for Petronella to solve her problem?
   a. Event 1
   b. Event 4
   c. Event 8

2. Why does Petronella ask the enchanter if she can work for him?
   a. She wants to help the old man.
   b. She wants to help the enchanter.
   c. She wants to rescue the prince.

3. When the enchanter warns Petronella that if she fails her task she must die, why does she say, "If I must, I must"?
   a. She is not very thrilled with the prince.
   b. She is already in love with the prince.
   c. She is afraid of Albion the enchanter.

4. Which sentence gives the correct order of events so far?
   a. Petronella is born, meets the enchanter, and frees the old man.
   b. Petronella meets the enchanter, then the old man, and then the prince.
   c. Petronella leaves home, frees the old man, and meets the prince.

5. Knowing what has happened so far, how do you predict Petronella might solve her problem?
   a. She will rescue Prince Ferdinand.
   b. She will give up quickly and go home.
   c. She will be rescued by Prince Ferdinand.

Comprehension Check

Review the tale if necessary. Then answer these questions:

1. Why don't the king and queen want Petronella to go out into the world?
   a. A princess isn't supposed to seek her fortune.
   b. A princess is supposed to seek her fortune.
   c. Petronella is too young to leave home.

2. Why has the old man been sitting at the divided road for sixty-two years?
   a. He's been confused and hasn't known which way to go.
   b. He's been waiting for someone to ask the right question.
   c. He's been waiting for someone to offer him a ride home.

3. What is unusual about Prince Ferdinand?
   a. He is lazy and selfish.
   b. He is suntanned and polite.
   c. He is brave and talented.

4. Why does Petronella want to work for the enchanter?
   a. If she works for the enchanter, she will earn a fortune.
   b. She wants to learn secrets that will help her save Ferdinand.
   c. The enchanter promised to train her to become an enchantress.

5. What is *not* an element of three in this tale?
   a. the sons of King Peter and Queen Blossom
   b. the place where the road divides
   c. the secrets Petronella wants from Albion

Check your answers with your teacher. Give yourself 1 point for each correct answer, and fill in your Strategy score here. Then turn to page 203 and transfer your score onto Graph 1.

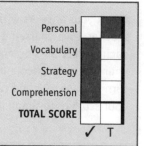

Personal
Vocabulary
Strategy
Comprehension
TOTAL SCORE
✓ T

Check your answers with your teacher. Give yourself 1 point for each correct answer, and fill in your Comprehension score here. Then turn to page 203 and transfer your score onto Graph 1.

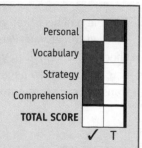

Personal
Vocabulary
Strategy
Comprehension
TOTAL SCORE
✓ T

Extending

Choose one or both of these activities:

PERFORM A FAIRY TALE

Choose a fairy tale that you brainstormed in Building Background or one of the tales listed on this page. Create a story map for the tale that includes the setting and characters, the problem, each of the important events, and the solution. Then use your story map to help you write the script for a puppet play or a short skit based on the tale. Invite other students to help you stage your performance. You may want to emphasize the elements of three in your production.

PREDICT PART 2 OF "PETRONELLA"

What do you predict might happen next in "Petronella"? Write the second part of this fairy tale. Before you begin writing, you may want to continue the story map in order to plan Part 2. Be sure to include a solution to Petronella's problem. Once you have finished writing Part 2, you may want to illustrate your fairy tale and post it with your classmates' tales to compare how each person solves Petronella's problem. After you finish reading the second part of this tale in Lesson 10, compare what happens in your class's versions to what happens in the real tale.

Resources

Books

Charles, Prince of Wales. *Old Man of Lochnagar.* Farar Straus & Giroux, 1980.

Dahl, Roald. *Esio Trot.* Viking, 1990.

Gerrard, Roy. *Sir Cedric.* Farrar Straus & Giroux, 1986.

Murphy, Jill. *Jeffrey Strangeways.* Candlewick Press, 1992.

Myers, Bernice. *Sidney Rella and the Glass Sneaker.* Macmillan, 1985.

Napoli, Donna Jo. *Prince of the Pond: Otherwise Known as De Fawg Pin.* Dutton, 1992.

Petronella (Part 2)

Building Background

From "Petronella" (Part 1):

At that moment the door of the house opened. Out came a man dressed all in black and silver. He was tall and thin, and his eyes were as black as a cloud full of thunder. Petronella knew at once that he must be the enchanter.

He bowed to her politely. "What can I do for you?"

"I wish to work for you," said Petronella boldly.

Albion nodded. "I cannot refuse you," he said. "But I warn you, it will be dangerous. Tonight I will give you a task. If you do it, I will reward you. If you fail, you must die."

Petronella glanced at the prince and sighed. "If I must, I must," she said. "Very well."

Read on to find out how things turn out in this modern fairy tale. Look for the elements of three in Part 2, and write them below.

Tales with Elements of Three

Title	How the Number Three Appears
"Petronella" (Part 2)	

Vocabulary Builder

1. The vocabulary words in the margin describe the animals in Part 2 of "Petronella." Use the words to complete these sentences:

   a. Another name for *dogs* is   _____.

   b. Another name for *horses* is   _____.

   c. Another name for *hawks* is   _____.

   d. Dogs bark, and horses   _____.

   e. Hawks have wings, but horses have   _____.

2. What do you predict the animals might do in this part of "Petronella"? Write your prediction in one or two sentences.

   _____

   _____

   _____

   _____.

3. Save your work. You will use it again in the Vocabulary Check.

bark

dogs

falcons

hawks

hoofs

horses

hounds

neigh

steeds

wings

Strategy Builder

Making Predictions While Reading

When you try to figure out what might happen next in a story, you are making a **prediction**. You can predict what might happen in Part 2 of "Petronella" by thinking about what happened in Part 1. Go back and read your Part 1 story maps for clues. Then, in the space below, write what you think might happen in Part 2. Don't worry if your predictions don't match what actually happens. You will have chances to make new ones at the Strategy Breaks.

I predict that in Part 2 of "Petronella," _____

_____

_____

_____

_____.

Petronella (Part 2)

by Jay Williams

Be looking for clues as you read to help you make predictions. Also keep looking for elements of three, and write them on your chart.

That evening they all had dinner together in the enchanter's cozy kitchen. Then Albion took Petronella out to a stone building and unbolted its door. Inside were seven huge black **dogs**.

"You must watch my **hounds** all night," said he.

Petronella went in, and Albion closed and locked the door.

At once the hounds began to snarl and **bark**. They bared their teeth at her. But Petronella was a real princess. She plucked up her courage. Instead of backing away, she went toward the dogs. She began to speak to them in a quiet voice. They stopped snarling and sniffed at her. She patted their heads.

"I see what it is," she said. "You are lonely here. I will keep you company."

And so all night long, she sat on the floor and talked to the hounds and stroked them. They lay close to her, panting.

In the morning, Albion came and let her out. "Ah," said he, "I see that you are brave. If you had run from the dogs, they would have torn you to pieces. Now you may ask for what you want."

"I want a comb for my hair," said Petronella.

The enchanter gave her a comb carved from a piece of black wood.

Prince Ferdinand was sunning himself and working at a crossword puzzle. Petronella said to him in a low voice, "I am doing this for you."

"That's nice," said the prince. "What's 'selfish' in nine letters?"

"You are," snapped Petronella. She went to the enchanter. "I will work for you once more," she said.

That night Albion led her to a stable. Inside were seven huge **horses**.

"Tonight," he said, "you must watch my **steeds**."

He went out and locked the door. At once the horses began to rear and **neigh**. They pawed at her with their iron **hoofs**.

But Petronella was a real princess. She looked closely at them and saw that their coats were rough and their manes and tails full of burrs.

"I see what it is," she said. "You are hungry and dirty."

She brought them as much hay as they could eat, and began to brush them. All night long she fed them and groomed them, and they stood quietly in their stalls.

In the morning Albion let her out. "You are as kind as you are brave," said he. "If you had run from them they would have trampled you under their hoofs. What will you have as a reward?"

"I want a mirror to look into," said Petronella.

The enchanter gave her a mirror made of silver.

She looked across the lawn at Prince Ferdinand. He was doing exercises leisurely. He was certainly handsome. She said to the enchanter, "I will work for you once more."

That night Albion led her to a loft above the stables. There, on perches, were seven great **hawks**.

"Tonight," said he, "you must watch my **falcons**."

As soon as Petronella was locked in, the hawks began to beat their **wings** and scream at her.

 Stop here for Strategy Break #1.

Strategy Break #1

1. What do you predict will happen next? _____
   _____

2. Why do you think so? _____
   _____

3. What clues from the tale helped you make your prediction?_____
   _____

 Go on reading to see what happens.

Petronella laughed. "That is not how birds sing," she said. "Listen."

She began to sing in a sweet voice. The hawks fell silent. All night long she sang to them, and they sat like feathered statues on their perches, listening.

In the morning Albion said, "You are as talented as you are kind and brave. If you had run from them, they would have pecked and clawed you without mercy. What do you want now?"

"I want a ring for my finger," said Petronella.

The enchanter gave her a ring made from a single diamond.

All that day and all that night Petronella slept, for she was very tired. But early the next morning, she crept into Prince Ferdinand's room. He was sound asleep, wearing purple pajamas.

"Wake up," whispered Petronella. "I am going to rescue you."

Ferdinand awoke and stared sleepily at her. "What time is it?"

"Never mind that," said Petronella. "Come on!"

"But I'm sleepy," Ferdinand objected. "And it's so pleasant here."

Petronella shook her head. "You're not much of a prince," she said grimly. "But you're the best I can do."

She grabbed him by the wrist and dragged him out of bed. She hauled him down the stairs. His horse and hers were in a separate stable, and she saddled them quickly. She gave the prince a shove, and he mounted. She jumped on her own horse, seized the prince's reins, and away they went like the wind.

They had not gone far when they heard a tremendous thumping. Petronella looked back. A dark cloud rose behind them, and beneath it she saw the enchanter. He was running with great strides, faster than the horses could go.

"What shall we do?" she cried.

"Don't ask me," said Prince Ferdinand grumpily. "I'm all shaken to bits by this fast riding."

Petronella desperately pulled out the comb. "The old man said this would help me!" she said. And because she didn't know what else to do with it, she threw the comb on the ground. At once a forest rose up. The trees were so thick that no one could get between them.

Away went Petronella and the prince. But the enchanter turned himself into an ax and began to chop. Right and left he chopped, slashing, and the trees fell before him.

Soon he was through the wood, and once again Petronella heard his footsteps thumping behind.

She reined in the horses. She took out the mirror and threw it on the ground. At once a wide lake spread out behind them, gray and glittering.

Off they went again. But the enchanter sprang into the water, turning himself into a salmon as he did so. He swam across the lake and leaped out of the water on to the other bank. Petronella heard him coming— *thump! thump!*—behind them again.

This time she threw down the ring. It didn't turn into anything, but lay shining on the ground.

The enchanter came running up. And as he jumped over the ring, it opened wide and then snapped up around him. It held his arms tight to his body, in a magical grip from which he could not escape.

"Well," said Prince Ferdinand, "that's the end of him."

Petronella looked at him in annoyance. Then she looked at the enchanter, held fast in the ring.

"Bother!" she said. "I can't just leave him here. He'll starve to death."

She got off her horse and went up to him. "If I release you," she said, "will you promise to let the prince go free?"

 Stop here for Strategy Break #2.

Strategy Break #2

1. Do your earlier predictions match what happened? _____ Why or why not? _____

2. What do you predict will happen next? _____ _____

3. Why do you think so? _____ _____

4. What clues from the tale helped you make your prediction? _____ _____

Go on reading to see what happens.

Albion stared at her in astonishment. "Let him go free?" he said. "What are you talking about? I'm glad to get rid of him."

It was Petronella's turn to look surprised. "I don't understand," she said. "Weren't you holding him prisoner?"

"Certainly not," said Albion. "He came to visit me for a weekend. At the end of it, he said, 'It's so pleasant here, do you mind if I stay on for another day or two?' I'm very polite and I said, 'Of course.' He stayed on, and on, and on. I didn't like to be rude to a guest and I couldn't just kick him out. I don't know what I'd have done if you hadn't dragged him away."

"But then—" said Petronella. "but then—why did you come running after him this way?"

"I wasn't chasing him," said the enchanter. "I was chasing *you*. You are just the girl I've been looking for. You are brave and kind and talented, and beautiful as well."

"Oh," said Petronella. "I see."

"Hmm," said she. "How do I get this ring off you?"

"Give me a kiss."

She did so. The ring vanished from around Albion and reappeared on Petronella's finger.

"I don't know what my parents will say when I come home with you instead of a prince," she said.

"Let's go and find out, shall we?" said the enchanter cheerfully.

He mounted one horse and Petronella the other. And off they trotted, side by side, leaving Prince Ferdinand of Firebright to walk home as best he could. ●

Strategy Follow-up

First go back and look at all the predictions you wrote in this lesson. Do any of them match what actually happened in this tale? Why or why not?

Next complete the following story map for Part 2 of "Petronella." Use another sheet of paper. Begin your story map with Event 9, and end with the solution. Some of the information has been filled in for you.

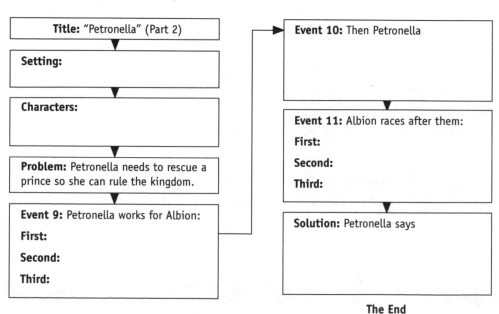

Title: "Petronella" (Part 2)

Setting:

Characters:

Problem: Petronella needs to rescue a prince so she can rule the kingdom.

Event 9: Petronella works for Albion:
First:
Second:
Third:

Event 10: Then Petronella

Event 11: Albion races after them:
First:
Second:
Third:

Solution: Petronella says

The End

✓Personal Checklist

Read each question and put a check (✓) in the correct box.

1   How well were you able to find the elements of three in this part of "Petronella"?

☐   3   (extremely well)

☐   2   (fairly well)

☐   1   (not well)

2.   How well were you able to complete the sentences in the Vocabulary Builder?

☐   3   (extremely well)

☐   2   (fairly well)

☐   1   (not well)

3.   How well were you able to predict what might happen in Part 2 of "Petronella"?

☐   3   (extremely well)

☐   2   (fairly well)

☐   1   (not well)

4.   How well do you understand why Albion runs after Petronella and Prince Ferdinand?

☐   3   (extremely well)

☐   2   (fairly well)

☐   1   (not well)

5.   How well do you understand why Petronella says, "I don't know what my parents will say when I come home with you instead of a prince"?

☐   3   (extremely well)

☐   2   (fairly well)

☐   1   (not well)

Vocabulary Check

Look back at the work you did in the Vocabulary Builder. Then answer each question by circling the correct letter.

1.   Which word describes the sound that horses make?

a. neigh

b. bark

c. screech

2.   Which two words describe the same animal?

a. *dogs* and *steeds*

b. *hawks* and *falcons*

c. *steeds* and *hounds*

3.   Which two words describe the same animal?

a. *hawks* and *steeds*

b. *steeds* and *horses*

c. *falcons* and *hounds*

4.   Which animals have hoofs (also called *hooves*)?

a. horses

b. steeds

c. both of the above

5.   Which animals have wings?

a. falcons

b. steeds

c. both of the above

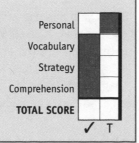

Add the numbers that you just checked to get your Personal Checklist score. Fill in your score here. Then turn to page 203 and transfer your score onto Graph 1.

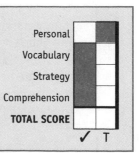

Check your answers with your teacher. Give yourself 1 point for each correct answer, and fill in your Vocabulary score here. Then turn to page 203 and transfer your score onto Graph 1.

Strategy Check

Look back at the predictions you wrote in this lesson. Then answer these questions:

1. In the Strategy Builder, if you had predicted that Petronella would succeed in her task, which clue would have best supported your prediction?

   a. Petronella has been brave and strong so far.

   b. Ferdinand is brave and will help Petronella.

   c. Albion seems nice and won't harm Petronella.

2. At Strategy Break #1, if you had predicted that Petronella would not run from the hawks, which clue would have best supported your prediction?

   a. There, on perches, were seven great hawks.

   b. The hawks began to scream at her.

   c. "If you had run from them they would have trampled you."

3. At Strategy Break #1, which prediction would *not* have fit this tale?

   a. Petronella will calm the hawks.

   b. Ferdinand will rescue Petronella from the hawks.

   c. Petronella will get a reward for watching the hawks.

4. At Strategy Break #2, if you had predicted the enchanter would let the prince go, which clue would have supported your prediction?

   a. He will punish Petronella for running.

   b. He will trick Petronella.

   c. He has been fair, so he will be fair again.

5. What might have been another clue that the enchanter would let the prince go free?

   a. Ferdinand is lazy and selfish, and the enchanter has no use for him.

   b. The enchanter enjoys Ferdinand's company and wants him around.

   c. The enchanter has a spell on Ferdinand that cannot be broken.

Comprehension Check

Review both parts of "Petronella" if necessary. Then answer these questions:

1. Which element makes this story a fairy tale?

   a. Petronella is a princess.

   b. Ferdinand is lazy and selfish.

   c. The enchanter turns himself into an ax.

2. What is an element of three in this tale?

   a. the number of things the enchanter gives Petronella

   b. the number of times the enchanter turns into something

   c. the number of falcons on perches in the loft

3. In what way are Petronella and Prince Ferdinand alike?

   a. They act like a typical prince and princess.

   b. They don't act like a typical prince and princess.

   c. They have very common first names.

4. Why does the enchanter run after Petronella and Ferdinand?

   a. He wants to take Ferdinand back.

   b. Petronella is just the girl he's been looking for.

   c. He wants to show how fast he can run.

5. Which sentence best sums up this tale?

   a. Nothing we ever really want is easy.

   b. That was the way it had always been.

   c. Petronella knew at once that he must be the enchanter.

Check your answers with your teacher. Give yourself 1 point for each correct answer, and fill in your Strategy score here. Then turn to page 203 and transfer your score onto Graph 1.

Personal
Vocabulary
Strategy
Comprehension
TOTAL SCORE
✓ T

Check your answers with your teacher. Give yourself 1 point for each correct answer, and fill in your Comprehension score here. Then turn to page 203 and transfer your score onto Graph 1.

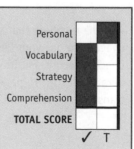

Personal
Vocabulary
Strategy
Comprehension
TOTAL SCORE
✓ T

Extending

Choose one or both of these activities:

DRAMATIZE "PETRONELLA"

"Petronella" is a wonderful tale to dramatize. Create a cast of characters and assign parts. Make a simple set by sketching the scene on the chalkboard, and dramatize the tale. You might have someone read the tale as others act it out. Or you might *ad lib*—make up the dialog as you go.

TEACH ANOTHER CLASS ABOUT FAIRY TALES

You learned quite a bit about fairy tales in Lessons 9 and 10. With a small group of classmates, make a poster that gives information about fairy tales. Include the elements often found in them, as well as examples of element of three. When you have finished your poster, check out some fairy tales from the library. The ones listed on this page are more modern. You might want to get a combination of modern and classic tales. Then use your poster to teach another class about fairy tales. Have members of your group take turns reading aloud from the library books. Stop every so often to point out the elements that make each story a fairy tale.

Resources

Books

Scieszka, Jon. *The Frog Prince, Continued.* Viking, 1991.

———. *The Stinky Cheese Man and Other Fairly Stupid Tales.* Viking, 1992.

Yolen, Jane. *The Giants' Farm.* New York Seabury Press, 1977.

———. *Sleeping Ugly.* Paper Star, 1997.

Learning New Words

Synonyms

A synonym is a word that means the same thing as another word. Author Jay Williams uses synonyms for some of the animals' names in "Petronella." For example, he calls the enchanter's dogs both *dogs* and *hounds.*

Draw a line from each word in Column 1 to its synonym in Column 2.

COLUMN 1	COLUMN 2
calm	giant
huge	argue
middle	gift
disagree	sparkle
shine	center
present	quiet

Antonyms

An antonym is a word that means the opposite of another word. The author of "Ostriches, or The Birds Nobody Noticed" uses the antonym pairs *fast* and *slow, ground* and *sky,* and *sunrise* and *sunset.*

Draw a line from each word in Column 1 to its antonym in Column 2.

COLUMN 1	COLUMN 2
question	end
difficult	easy
thick	dirty
clean	thin
weak	answer
begin	strong

Suffixes

A suffix is a word part that is added to the end of a word. When you add a suffix, you often change the word's meaning and function. For example, adding the suffix *-less* to the word *sense* changes the noun *sense* to an adjective meaning "without sense."

-ful

The suffix *-ful* means "full of." The mule in *Grandaddy's Place* became *thoughtful,* or "full of thought," after the star hopped on its back.

Write the word that each definition describes.

1. full of joy   _____

2. full of pain   _____

3. full of hope   _____

4. full of cheer   _____

-able

The suffix *-able* means "able to be _____ed." When Petronella's brother Michael asks her to be *reasonable,* he wants her to be "able to be reasoned with."

Write the definition of each word.

1. enjoyable _____

2. reachable _____

3. mailable _____

4. watchable _____

-er

The suffix *-er* is a special kind of suffix. It turns a word into a noun that means "a person who _____." In "Petronella," you learned that an *enchanter* is a person who enchants, or uses magic.

Now write the word that describes each person below.

1. a person who sings   _____

2. a person who writes   _____

3. a person who paints   _____

4. a person who teaches   _____

5. a person who dances   _____

VOCABULARY

From Lesson 6
- thoughtful

From Lesson 9
- reasonable

From Lesson 9
- enchanter

The Pudding Like a Night on the Sea

Building Background

Imagine that your friend Bill told you, "Julian got carried away last night!" Would you understand what Bill meant? Maybe someone picked Julian up and carried him away. Maybe Julian did too much of something—like made too much noise or ate too much.

To understand what Bill really meant, you need information. Where was Julian? What was he doing? Whom was he with? What kind of person is Julian? Without this information, you might misunderstand Bill.

Misunderstandings usually happen when you don't know enough about a person or situation. Misunderstandings also happen when information is taken out of context. **Context** is information that comes before and after a word or a situation to help you understand it.

The following exercise will help you understand how context works.

1. Write this sentence at the top of a sheet of paper:

   That was a blast!

2. Think of one meaning for the sentence. On the top half of the paper, write or draw the context that would help someone understand your meaning.

3. Then think of another meaning for the sentence.

4. On the bottom half of the paper, write or draw the context that would help someone understand that meaning.

5. Explain why someone might misunderstand the sentence if the context was not clear.

beat

whip

Vocabulary Builder

1. Before you begin reading "The Pudding Like a Night on the Sea," write down all the meanings of *beat* and *whip* that you know. (Use the clipboards on the right and a dictionary if you need to.)

3. Later, as you read the story, decide which of the meanings that you wrote for *beat* and *whip* match the meanings used in the story. Put a star (★) next to those meanings.

4. Save your work. You will use it again in the Vocabulary Check.

CLIPBOARD

beat

Strategy Builder

Making Predictions While Reading a Story

- When you read, you often make predictions. As you know, a **prediction** is a kind of guess. To make a prediction, act like a detective. Use the story's most important information, or clues, to figure out what will happen next.

- The clues in a story are sometimes called its context. Remember that **context** is information that comes before or after a word or situation to help you understand it better.

- As you read "The Pudding Like a Night on the Sea," you will pause twice to make predictions. At each pause, write down which context clues helped you make your prediction. Also tell why the story is or is not turning out the way you predicted it would.

CLIPBOARD

whip

The Pudding Like a Night on the Sea

by Ann Cameron

The story you are about to read shows why the right context is important—and how misunderstandings can happen without it.

"I'm going to make something special for your mother," my father said.

My mother was out shopping. My father was in the kitchen, looking at the pots and the pans and jars of this and that.

"What are you going to make?" I said.

"A pudding," he said.

My father is a big man with wild black hair. When he laughs, the sun laughs in the windowpanes. When he thinks, you can almost see his thoughts sitting on all the tables and chairs. When he is angry, me and my little brother Huey shiver to the bottom of our shoes.

"What kind of pudding will you make?" Huey said.

"A wonderful pudding," my father said. "It will taste like a whole raft of lemons. It will taste like a night on the sea."

Then he took down a knife and sliced five lemons in half. He squeezed the first one. Juice squirted in my eye.

"Stand back!" he said, and squeezed again. The seeds flew out on the floor. "Pick up those seeds, Huey!" he said.

Huey took the broom and swept them up.

My father cracked some eggs and put the yolks in a pan and the whites in a bowl. He rolled up his sleeves and pushed back his hair and **beat** up the yolks. "Sugar, Julian!" he said, and I poured in the sugar.

He went on beating. Then he put in lemon juice and cream and set the pan on the stove. The pudding bubbled and he stirred it fast. Cream splashed on the stove.

"Wipe that up, Huey!" he said.

Huey did.

It was hot by the stove. My father loosened his collar and pushed at his sleeves. The stuff in the pan was getting thicker and thicker. He held the beater up high in the air. "Just right!" he said, and sniffed in the smell of the pudding.

He **whipped** the egg whites and mixed them into the pudding. The pudding looked softer and lighter than air.

"Done!" he said. He washed all the pots, splashing water on the floor, and wiped the counter so fast his hair made circles around his head.

"Perfect!" he said. "Now I'm going to take a nap. If something important happens, bother me. If nothing important happens, don't bother me. And—the pudding is for your mother. Leave the pudding alone!"

He went to the living room and was asleep in a minute, sitting straight up in his chair.

Huey and I guarded the pudding.

 Stop here for Strategy Break #1.

Strategy Break #1

1. What do you predict will happen next? _____
    _____

2. Why do you think so? _____
    _____

3. What clues from the story helped you make your prediction? _____
    _____
    _____

Go on reading to see what happens.

"Oh, it's a wonderful pudding," Huey said.

"With waves on top like the ocean," I said.

"I wonder how it tastes," Huey said.

"Leave the pudding alone," I said.

"If I just put my finger in—there—I'll know how it tastes," Huey said. And he did it.

"You did it!" I said. "How does it taste?"

"It tastes like a whole raft of lemons," he said. "It tastes like a night on the sea."

"You've made a hole in the pudding!" I said. "But since you did it, I'll have a taste." And it tasted like a whole night of lemons. It tasted like floating at sea.

"It's such a big pudding," Huey said. "It can't hurt to have a little more."

"Since you took more, I'll have more," I said.

"That was a bigger lick than I took!" Huey said. "I'm going to have more again."

"Whoops!" I said.

"You put in your whole hand!" Huey said. "Look at the pudding you spilled on the floor!"

"I am going to clean it up," I said. And I took the rag from the sink.

"That's not really clean," Huey said.

"It's the best I can do," I said.

"Look at the pudding!" Huey said.

It looked like craters on the moon. "We have to smooth this over," I said. "So it looks the way it did before! Let's get spoons."

And we evened the top of the pudding with spoons, and while we evened it, we ate some more.

"There isn't much left," I said.

"We were supposed to leave the pudding alone," Huey said.

"We'd better get away from here," I said. We ran into our bedroom and crawled under the bed. After a long time we heard my father's voice.

"Come into the kitchen, dear," he said. "I have something for you."

"Why, what is it?" my mother said, out in the kitchen.

Under the bed, Huey and I pressed ourselves to the wall.

"Look," said my father, out in the kitchen. "A wonderful pudding."

"Where is the pudding?" my mother said.

"WHERE ARE YOU BOYS?" my father said. His voice went through every crack and corner of the house.

We felt like two leaves in a storm.

"WHERE ARE YOU? I SAID!" my father's voice was booming.

Huey whispered to me, "I'm scared."

We heard my father walking slowly through the rooms.

"Huey!" he called. "Julian!"

We could see his feet. He was coming into our room.

He lifted the bedspread. There was his face, and his eyes like black lightning. He grabbed us by the legs and pulled. "STAND UP!" he said.

We stood.

"What do you have to tell me?" he said.

"We went outside," Huey said, "and when we came back, the pudding was gone!"

"Then why are you hiding under the bed?" my father said.

We didn't say anything. We looked at the floor.

"I can tell you one thing," he said. There is going to be some **beating** here now! There is going to be some **whipping**!"

The curtains at the window were shaking. Huey was holding my hand.

"Go into the kitchen!" my father said. "Right now!"

We went into the kitchen.

"Come here, Huey!" my father said.

 Stop here for Strategy Break #2.

Strategy Break #2

1. Do your earlier predictions match what happened? _____ Why or why not? _____
   _____
   _____

2. What do you predict will happen next? _____
   _____

3. Why do you think so? _____
   _____

4. What clues from the story helped you make your prediction? _____
   _____

➡ **Go on reading to see what happens.**

Huey walked toward him, his hands behind his back.

"See these eggs?" my father said. He cracked them and put the yolks in a pan and set the pan on the counter. He stood a chair by the counter. "Stand up here," he said to Huey.

Huey stood on the chair by the counter.

"Now it's time for your beating!" my father said.

Huey started to cry. His tears fell in with the egg yolks.

"Take this!" my father said. My father handed him the egg beater. "Now beat those eggs," he said. "I want this to be a good beating!"

"Oh!" Huey said. He stopped crying. And he beat the egg yolks.

"Now you, Julian, stand here!" my father said.

I stood on a chair by the table.

"I hope you're ready for your whipping!"

I didn't answer. I was afraid to say yes or no.

"Here!" he said, and he set the egg whites in front of me. "I want these whipped and whipped well!"

"Yes, sir!" I said, and started whipping.

My father watched us. My mother came into the kitchen and watched us.

After a while Huey said, "This is hard work."

"That's too bad," my father said. "Your beating's not done!" And he added sugar and cream and lemon juice to Huey's pan and put the pan on the stove. And Huey went on beating.

"My arm hurts from whipping," I said.

"That's too bad," my father said. "Your whipping's not done."

So I whipped and whipped, and Huey beat and beat.

"Hold that beater in the air, Huey!" my father said.

Huey held it in the air.

"See!" my father said. "A good pudding stays on the beater. It's thick enough now. Your beating's done." Then he turned to me. "Let's see those egg whites, Julian!" he said. They were puffed up and fluffy. "Congratulations Julian!" he said. "Your whipping's done."

He mixed the egg whites into the pudding himself. Then he passed the pudding to my mother.

"A wonderful pudding," she said. "Would you like some, boys?"

"No thank you," we said.

She picked up a spoon. "Why, this tastes like a whole raft of lemons," she said. "This tastes like a night on the sea." ●

Strategy Follow-up

Go back and look at the predictions that you wrote in this lesson. Do any of them match what actually happened in this story? Why or why not?

✓Personal Checklist

Read each question and put a check (✓) in the correct box.

1. How well do you understand what happened in "The Pudding Like a Night on the Sea"?
   - ☐ 3 (extremely well)
   - ☐ 2 (fairly well)
   - ☐ 1 (not well)

2. How well do you understand what the boys' father was like?
   - ☐ 3 (extremely well)
   - ☐ 2 (fairly well)
   - ☐ 1 (not well)

3. How well were you able to use the information in Building Background to figure out the misunderstanding in this story?
   - ☐ 3 (extremely well)
   - ☐ 2 (fairly well)
   - ☐ 1 (not well)

4. How well were you able to use the definitions of *beat* and *whip* to figure out the misunderstanding in this story?
   - ☐ 3 (extremely well)
   - ☐ 2 (fairly well)
   - ☐ 1 (not well)

5. How well were you able to predict what would happen next in this story?
   - ☐ 3 (extremely well)
   - ☐ 2 (fairly well)
   - ☐ 1 (not well)

Vocabulary Check

Look back at the work you did in the Vocabulary Builder. Then answer each question by circling the correct letter.

1. When the boys' father said, "There is going to be some beating here now! There is going to be some whipping!" why do you think the boys misunderstood him?
   a. They had disobeyed him, so they thought he was going to punish them.
   b. They were thinking of different meanings for *beat* and *whip* than the meanings their father was using.
   c. Both of the above answers are correct.

2. Which meaning of *whip* were the boys thinking of?
   a. "hit with a stick or a lash"
   b. "stir quickly to make a foam"
   c. "sew stitches over the edge of a cloth"

3. Which meaning of *beat* was their father thinking of?
   a. "defeat or overcome"
   b. "mark time in music by tapping or clapping"
   c. "mix with a fork or a spoon"

4. Which context was the boys' father using when he said there was going to be some beating?
   a. the context of drumming
   b. the context of baking
   c. the context of punishment

5. Which context did the *boys* think their father was using when he said there was going to be some beating?
   a. the context of drumming
   b. the context of baking
   c. the context of punishment

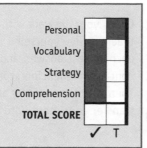

Add the numbers that you just checked to get your Personal Checklist score. Fill in your score here. Then turn to page 203 and transfer your score onto Graph 1.

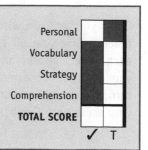

Check your answers with your teacher. Give yourself 1 point for each correct answer, and fill in your Vocabulary score here. Then turn to page 203 and transfer your score onto Graph 1.

Strategy Check

Look back at what you wrote at each Strategy Break. Then answer these questions:

1. At Strategy Break #1, if you had predicted that the boys would obey their father, which clue would have best supported your prediction?
   a. "Just right!" he said, and sniffed in the smell.
   b. Huey and I guarded the pudding.
   c. "Now I'm going to take a nap."

2. If you had predicted that the boys would disobey their father, which clue would have best supported your prediction?
   a. "And—the pudding is for your mother. Leave the pudding alone!"
   b. "If nothing important happens, don't bother me."
   c. When he laughs, the sun laughs in the windowpanes.

3. At Strategy Break #2, which prediction would *not* have fit the story?
   a. The boys' father will not punish them.
   b. The boy's father will be very angry with them.
   c. The boys' father will punish them.

4. At Strategy Break #2, if you had predicted that the boys' father would punish them, which clue would have best supported your prediction?
   a. "Look," said my father, . . . "A wonderful pudding."
   b. "It's such a big pudding, . . . it can't hurt to have a little more."
   c. "WHERE ARE YOU BOYS?" my father said.

5. Which clue explains what the boys' father meant when he said, "There is going to be some beating here now!"
   a. "Stand up here," he said to Huey.
   b. "Now it's time for your beating!"
   c. "Now beat those eggs," he said.

Comprehension Check

Review the story if necessary. Then answer these questions:

1. What was the misunderstanding in the story?
   a. The boys didn't understand what their father meant by "beating" and "whipping."
   b. The boys didn't understand that they were not to touch the pudding.
   c. The boys didn't understand how pudding could taste like a raft of lemons and a night on the sea.

2. How might the misunderstanding have been avoided?
   a. The boys could have asked their father if they could eat the pudding.
   b. The boys' father could have held up the eggbeater and eggs.
   c. The boys' father could have described the pudding another way.

3. How did Julian and Huey "get carried away"?
   a. Their father carried them to bed.
   b. They meant to just taste the pudding but ended up eating most of it.
   c. They made a big mess while they were helping their father make the pudding.

4. Which words best describe the boys' father?
   a. angry and mean
   b. serious and boring
   c. loving and fair

5. What might "a whole raft of lemons and a night on the sea" taste like?
   a. as lemony as the juice of a whole raft of lemons and as smooth as the sea at night
   b. like hard and chewy pieces of lemon floating in a watery pudding
   c. as woody as the bark of a raft that was floating on the sea at night

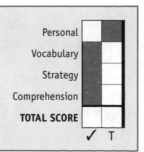

Check your answers with your teacher. Give yourself 1 point for each correct answer, and fill in your Strategy score here. Then turn to page 203 and transfer your score onto Graph 1.

Personal
Vocabulary
Strategy
Comprehension
TOTAL SCORE
✓ T

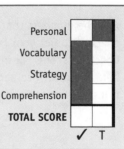

Check your answers with your teacher. Give yourself 1 point for each correct answer, and fill in your Comprehension score here. Then turn to page 203 and transfer your score onto Graph 1.

Personal
Vocabulary
Strategy
Comprehension
TOTAL SCORE
✓ T

Extending
Choose one or more of these activities:

WRITE ABOUT A MISUNDERSTANDING
Write a story about characters who misunderstand each other because of the words they use. Be sure your story tells (1) how the misunderstanding happens, (2) what problems it causes, and (3) how the misunderstanding and the problems are solved. You may want to ask a few classmates to help you dramatize your story for the rest of the class.

MAKE A PUDDING
Find a pudding recipe that tells you to whip and/or beat the ingredients. (If the cookbook you use has definitions for *whip* and *beat*, add them to the list you made in the Vocabulary Builder.) Make the pudding and share it with family or friends.

PUDDING LIKE . . .
The pudding in this story tasted like "a whole raft of lemons and a night on the sea." After you taste the pudding you have made, write five phrases that describe it. Begin each phrase with the words "Pudding like _____." (If you didn't make any pudding, make each phrase describe your favorite pudding.)

Resources
Books
Darling, Jennifer Dorland, ed. *Better Homes and Gardens New Junior Cookbook*. Meredith Books, 1997.

Kilpatrick, James J. *The Ear Is Human: A Handbook of Homophones and Other Confusions*. Andrews McMeel Publishing, 1985.

Manus, Gerald I., and Muriel R. Manus. *Phonic Foolers: A Creative Arts Dictionary of Homophones*. Creative Arts Book Company, 1998.

Web Site
http://www.recipesource.com/side-dishes/puddings
This Web site contains hundreds of pudding recipes, arranged in alphabetical order.

Flash, Crash, Rumble, and Roll

Building Background

What is the weather like today? Is the sun shining? Is it snowing? Or is it raining where you are? In the article you are about to read, you will learn what causes thunder and lightning. You and your classmates probably know some things about thunder and lightning already. Get together and list what you know.

electricity

expands

ice crystal

sound waves

spark

water vapor

Vocabulary Builder

1. In Lesson 8, you learned that **specialized vocabulary** words all relate to the topic of a particular selection. For example, in "What Makes a Bird a Bird?" the specialized vocabulary words *call, chicks, camouflaged, molt, nest,* and *preen* all relate to the topic of birds.

2. Draw a line from each specialized vocabulary word in Column 1 to its definition in Column 2. Then think about how each word might be used in an article about thunder and lightning.

COLUMN 1	COLUMN 2
electricity	solid shape that forms when water freezes
expands	water in the form of gas
ice crystal	the way in which sounds travel
sound waves	spreads out or gets bigger
spark	form of energy that can cause sparks
water vapor	flash created when electricity jumps across an open space

3. Save your work. You will use it again in the Vocabulary Check.

Strategy Builder

Identifying Sequence When You Read

- When writers describe the process of how something works or is made, they describe the steps in order. That order is called **sequence**.

- To make the sequence as clear as possible, writers often use signal words. **Signal words** help you get a more exact picture of when things happen. Some examples of signal words are *first, next, then, finally,* and *after a while.*

- See if you can follow the sequence of events in the paragraphs below. Use the underlined signal words to help you.

"There's a strong storm moving in from the west," said the radio announcer. "Better head undercover before it hits your area."

Upon hearing the radio report, the lifeguards blew their whistles and got everyone out of the pool. <u>Then</u> they moved everyone into the changing rooms. <u>Next</u>, they closed the umbrellas and tipped the chairs so the wind would not blow them away.

<u>After the storm passed</u>, the guards blew three long whistles, and everyone jumped back into the pool. The splash they made was almost as loud as the thunder.

- If you wanted to keep track of the sequence of events in these paragraphs, you could put them on a **sequence chain**. It might look like this:

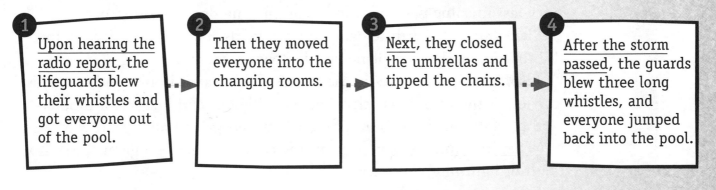

Flash, Crash, Rumble, and Roll

by Franklyn M. Branley

As you read the first part of this article, you can apply the strategies that you just learned. Notice the underlined signal words. They will give you a more exact picture of the sequence of events.

The day is quiet. The air is still and hot, leaves do not move, flowers droop, and even the birds are still and quiet.

There are big white clouds in the sky. They grow bigger and taller, and they get darker and darker.

"Look at those black thunderclouds," people say. "We're going to have a thunderstorm."

Warm air near the earth is rising into the clouds. The air goes up fast, and inside the clouds it keeps moving upward. It may go all the way to the top and spill over.

The clouds keep growing. <u>After a while</u> the clouds may be ten miles high.

The rising air carries water, but it's not liquid. It is a gas called **water vapor**. <u>When water vapor cools</u>, it becomes liquid water and changes into small drops of water or into small crystals of ice. That's what happens in the clouds to make them grow.

Air inside the clouds carries the water and ice up and up. The air gets colder and colder. <u>When it gets very cold</u>, the air falls. So air is moving up very fast in some parts of a cloud and moving down in other parts.

Planes stay out of these dark thunderclouds. The rushing air is so forceful that it could turn a plane upside down.

Also, there's **electricity** in the clouds. Each water droplet and **ice crystal** carries a tiny bit of electricity. There are billions and billions of droplets and crystals. So the amount of electricity gets greater and greater.

<u>When the amount is very great</u>, the electricity makes a giant **spark**—a flash of lightning!

Rain starts to fall. First only a drop or two, then the wind blows, and the rain falls faster and harder. Water races down the street.

There's more lightning. It may go from one cloud to another, or it may reach a high building or a tree. The streak of lightning may be a mile long, or even longer.

Stop here for the Strategy Break.

Strategy Break

If you were to create a sequence chain to show what causes lightning, it might look like this:

1 Warm air rises into the clouds, and they keep growing. <u>After a while</u> they may be ten miles high.

2 Air in the clouds carries water vapor up. <u>When water vapor cools</u>, it becomes liquid, which changes into ice. This is what makes the clouds grow.

3 The air in the clouds gets colder and colder. <u>When it gets very cold</u>, the air falls. So air is moving up in some parts of the cloud and down in others.

4 The electricity in the clouds gets greater and greater. <u>When the amount is very great</u>, the electricity makes a giant spark— lightning.

As you continue reading, keep paying attention to the sequence of events. Also keep looking for signal words. At the end of this article, you will use some of them to create a sequence chain of your own.

 Go on reading.

Thunder comes after the lightning. The lightning is very hot. It heats the air, and the hot air **expands** very fast. It makes **sound waves** all along the streak of lightning.

The sound waves reach you at different times. When the first one reaches your ears, there may be a loud crash. As more and more sound waves reach you, the thunder rumbles and rolls.

You make sound waves when you break a balloon. Blow one up and pop it. The air in the balloon expands rapidly through the break in the skin. You made a tiny bit of thunder. There's only a little air in a balloon, so there's not much noise. Lightning moves lots more air—billions of times more—so there is a big noise.

Sound waves travel slowly, much more slowly than the light from lightning.

Light travels so fast, it can go to the moon in less than two seconds. It would take two weeks for sound to go that far.

Because light goes so fast, you see lightning the moment it flashes. But it may take several seconds for the thunder to reach you. It takes five seconds for the sound to travel one mile.

The next time you see lightning, try this: Count the seconds until you hear the thunder. If five seconds go by, the storm is one mile away. If ten seconds pass, the storm is two miles away. If only a second passes, the storm is very close. The thunder will be very loud. It may be scary, but thunder won't hurt you.

Lightning is different. It may start fires in houses or barns or forests. It may knock over trees and telephone poles or it may kill cows and horses in a field. It may also hurt or even kill people. But you won't be hurt by lightning if you know what to do.

If you are swimming, *get out of the water.*

If you are outside, *go inside.*

If you are inside when a storm is close, *stay away* from the telephone and the TV. Their wires could carry lightning into the house.

Stay away from the stove and other big metal things.

Stay away from sinks, the bathtub, and the shower. Their pipes could also carry lightning into the house.

If you are caught outdoors, *keep away* from metal fences or metal pipes. They could carry electricity.

Don't stand under a tree that is alone in a field. Lightning usually strikes the highest thing. It might strike the tree. *Don't be the highest thing* around in a big field. Crouch down with your knees on the ground and bend your head forward.

If you are in a car, *stay there.* A car is safe because if lightning hits it, the electricity goes through the car and not through you.

Watch the storm from a safe place. Before it begins, watch the clouds. You'll see them get bigger and bigger, taller and taller, darker and darker. You'll see flashes of lightning. If the storm is far away, you'll hear thunder rumble and roll. If it's close by, the thunder will crackle and crash.

People used to think that lightning was the fiery finger of an angry god. They thought the god made thunder when he scolded and roared. They feared storms as much as they feared their gods.

But there's no reason to fear storms. If you understand what makes thunder and lightning, you'll know how to keep safe. ●

Strategy Follow-up

On a separate sheet of paper, create a sequence chain that describes what causes thunder. Underline the signal words.

✓Personal Checklist

Read each question and put a check (✓) in the correct box.

1. In Building Background, how easily were you able to list what you know about thunder and lightning?
   - ☐ 3 (extremely easily)
   - ☐ 2 (fairly easily)
   - ☐ 1 (not easily)

2. In the Vocabulary Builder, how well were you able to match the specialized vocabulary words with their definitions?
   - ☐ 3 (extremely well)
   - ☐ 2 (fairly well)
   - ☐ 1 (not well)

3. How well were you able to create a sequence chain in the Strategy Follow-up?
   - ☐ 3 (extremely well)
   - ☐ 2 (fairly well)
   - ☐ 1 (not well)

4. How well do you understand the information in this article?
   - ☐ 3 (extremely well)
   - ☐ 2 (fairly well)
   - ☐ 1 (not well)

5. After reading this article, how well would you be able to tell people how to protect themselves from lightning?
   - ☐ 3 (extremely well)
   - ☐ 2 (fairly well)
   - ☐ 1 (not well)

Vocabulary Check

Look back at the work you did in the Vocabulary Builder. Then answer each question by circling the correct letter.

1. Which definition of *spark* is used in this article?
   - a. electric flash
   - b. small amount
   - c. small bit of fire

2. Which word best defines *water vapor*?
   - a. solid
   - b. liquid
   - c. gas

3. Which phrase best defines lightning?
   - a. spurts of hot air
   - b. flashes of electricity
   - c. rolling sound waves

4. What happens to clouds when ice crystals form in them?
   - a. They start to shrink.
   - b. They start to expand.
   - c. They start to break apart.

5. How does sound travel?
   - a. as waves
   - b. through electricity
   - c. over lightning bolts

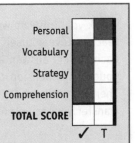

Add the numbers that you just checked to get your Personal Checklist score. Fill in your score here. Then turn to page 203 and transfer your score onto Graph 1.

Personal
Vocabulary
Strategy
Comprehension
TOTAL SCORE
✓ T

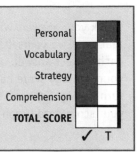

Check your answers with your teacher. Give yourself 1 point for each correct answer, and fill in your Vocabulary score here. Then turn to page 203 and transfer your score onto Graph 1.

Personal
Vocabulary
Strategy
Comprehension
TOTAL SCORE
✓ T

Strategy Check

Look back at the sequence chain that you completed in the Strategy Follow-up. Then answer these questions:

1. According to the article, when does thunder happen?
   a. before lightning
   b. after lightning
   c. before rain falls

2. What happens just before you hear thunder?
   a. Clouds keep growing.
   b. Clouds move fast.
   c. Lightning heats the air.

3. How do thunder's sound waves reach you?
   a. all at one time
   b. at different times
   c. through phone lines

4. Why do you hear thunder after you see lightning?
   a. Light travels much more slowly than sound.
   b. Sound travels much more quickly than light.
   c. Sound travels much more slowly than light.

5. Which sentence gives the wrong sequence?
   a. Lightning strikes, ice crystals form, and warm air rises.
   b. Warm air rises, lightning strikes, and thunder claps.
   c. Cold air falls, electricity builds, and lightning strikes.

Comprehension Check

Review the article if necessary. Then answer these questions:

1. Why do planes stay out of thunderclouds?
   a. The forceful air could turn a plane upside down.
   b. The thunder is so loud it could make people deaf.
   c. The air is so cold it could freeze the plane.

2. How can you tell how far away lightning is?
   a. Count how many seconds the lightning lasts.
   b. Count the seconds until you hear the thunder.
   c. Count the minutes until you hear the thunder.

3. When there is lightning outside, why should you stay away from the TV?
   a. Its picture can start to change color.
   b. Its wires can carry lightning into the house.
   c. Its channels can carry lightning into the house.

4. What else should you do to be safe from lightning?
   a. Stand in a big open field.
   b. If you're in a car, get out of it.
   c. Stay away from big metal things.

5. What did people think thunder was long ago?
   a. the fiery finger of an angry god
   b. the sound of the god bowling in heaven
   c. the sound the god made when angry

Check your answers with your teacher. Give yourself 1 point for each correct answer, and fill in your Strategy score here. Then turn to page 203 and transfer your score onto Graph 1.

Personal
Vocabulary
Strategy
Comprehension
TOTAL SCORE
✓ T

Check your answers with your teacher. Give yourself 1 point for each correct answer, and fill in your Comprehension score here. Then turn to page 203 and transfer your score onto Graph 1.

Personal
Vocabulary
Strategy
Comprehension
TOTAL SCORE
✓ T

Extending

Choose one or both of these activities:

EXPLAIN THE WEATHER

Choose a particular kind of storm, such as a hurricane, a blizzard, or a tornado. Using some of the resources on this page or others, find information about your chosen storm. Prepare a short report, and present it to the rest of the class as though you were an announcer on a weather channel or the nightly news. Explain how this kind of storm develops and what people can do to protect themselves from it.

RESEARCH EL NIÑO

El Niño is a storm system that causes weather changes throughout the world. Find information on *El Niño*, such as when and how often it occurs and how it affects the world. If you can, interview farmers, fishermen, or other people who depend on the weather for their work and income. See how *El Niño* has affected them and their work.

Resources

Books

Arnold, Caroline. *El Niño: Stormy Weather for People and Wildlife.* Clarion Books, 1998.

Berger, Melvin. *How's the Weather? A Look at Weather and How It Changes.* Ideals Children's Books, 1993.

Branley, Franklyn. *Flash, Crash, Rumble, and Roll.* HarperCollins, 1999.

Engelbert, Phillis. *Complete Weather Resource.* UXL, 1997.

Kramer, Stephen P. *Eye of the Storm: Chasing Storms with Warren Faidley.* G. P. Putnam's Sons, 1997.

Simon, Seymour. *Storms.* Morrow Junior Books, 1989.

Web Sites

http://www.elnino.noaa.gov
The National Oceanic and Atmospheric Administration gives information on El Niño and its worldwide effects.

http://www.lightningsafety.com
The National Lightning Safety Institute provides information on keeping safe during storms.

On Bicycles

Building Background

You probably know quite a bit about bicycles already. You probably have seen many different kinds and know what they are used for. As you read *On Bicycles,* you will be adding to your knowledge by learning about bicycle safety.

There might be some specialized vocabulary words about bicycles in this selection that are new to you. To figure out what the words mean, you can use the definitions, examples, and explanations given in the text. These hints are called **context clues**.

bell

brakes

frame

handlebars

horn

light

pedals

rearview mirror

reflector

seat

spokes

tire

Vocabulary Builder

1. Use the specialized vocabulary words in the margin to make a diagram of a bicycle.

2. First, draw a bicycle in the box below. Then label it with the vocabulary words. Use an encyclopedia or other source if you need help.

3. Save your work. You will use it again in the Vocabulary Check.

Diagram of a Bicycle

Strategy Builder

Outlining Main Ideas and Supporting Details

- You already know that most informational writing describes a particular **topic**, such as dogs or birds or bicycles.

- You also know that most informational writing is organized according to **main ideas** and **supporting details**. These ideas and details help explain or support the topic.

- There are many ways to keep track of main ideas and details as you read. One way is to make a simple **outline**. Outlines can be helpful as you do research, plan your own writing, or study for a test.

- Read the following simple outline. It is for part of the selection "Flash, Crash, Rumble, and Roll." Notice how the main ideas are numbered and the details have letters.

Flash, Crash, Rumble, and Roll

1. Lightning
   a. Warm air rises, carrying water vapor.
   b. Water vapor cools and turns into ice crystals.
   c. Electricity builds in water droplets and ice crystals.
   d. Electricity sparks to make lightning.

2. Thunder
   a. Lightning heats the air.
   b. The air expands.
   c. The expanding air makes the sound waves that we hear as thunder.

On Bicycles

by Kyle Carter

As you read this selection, notice how it is organized. Think about how you might show the main ideas and supporting details on a simple outline.

BICYCLE SAFETY

Riding a bicycle is great fun and exercise. Still, riding a bicycle can be dangerous. Each year many bicycle riders are injured or killed.

As a bicycle rider, you have little protection if an accident happens. Knowing how to ride a bike safely can help you avoid accidents.

THE RIGHT BIKE

A bike won't quite fit you like a glove. Your bike can—and should—fit you well.

A good fit is important for safe riding. You should be able to touch your feet to the ground while standing astride the bike **frame**. If you can't do that, the bike is too big.

A big bike is the wrong bike. You are much more likely to fall from a bike that's too big.

CHECK IT OUT

If the bike fits, check its condition. The **handlebars** need to be tight. The **seat** needs to be tight and set in a comfortable position. The **brakes** need to work well.

If a **tire** looks worn or has begun to leak, have it replaced.

Grease and oil keep certain parts of the bike moving smoothly. You can lubricate—grease and oil—your own bike after someone shows you how.

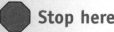 **Stop here for the Strategy Break.**

Strategy Break

If you were to make a simple outline for what you've read so far, it might look like the one below. Notice that the main ideas are the headings from each section. The details from each section support the main ideas.

On Bicycles

1. Bicycle Safety
   a. Each year, many bicycle riders are injured or killed.
   b. Knowing how to ride safely can help you avoid accidents.
2. The Right Bike
   a. Your bike should fit you well.
   b. If you can't touch your feet to the ground while standing, the bike is too big.
   c. You're much more likely to fall from a bike that's too big.
3. Check It Out
   a. Handlebars need to be tight.
   b. Seat needs to be tight and comfortable.
   c. Brakes need to work well.
   d. Worn or leaking tires need to be replaced.
   e. Bike parts need to be lubricated (greased and oiled).

As you continue reading, keep paying attention to the main ideas and supporting details. At the end of this selection, you will use some of them to complete an outline of your own.

 Go on reading.

RULES OF THE ROAD

If you ride a bike on the street, you are part of the traffic. Even as a bicyclist, you must obey traffic rules.

That means you must ride on the right, moving in the same direction as cars and trucks.

You must obey road signs and traffic signals. Be especially careful at intersections, the places where one street joins another.

PLAYING IT SAFE

You can do many things to ride your bike more safely. If you and a friend are riding bikes, always ride in single file. That gives cars more room to pass you. Never ride with two people on a one-seat bike.

Equip your bike with a **horn** or loud **bell**. Also, equip your bike or your safety helmet with a **rearview mirror**.

SIGNATURE READING, D

HELMETS

One of the most important things you can do is wear a safety helmet. A helmet, carefully fit to your head, can help save you from serious injury.

Bicycle helmets are light but strong. In case of an accident, let the helmet take the beating instead of your head!

USING YOUR HANDS

You need to keep your bike under control at all times. That requires careful and constant attention. It also requires both hands on the handlebars.

If you are making a turn in traffic, however, you need to use your left arm to signal. Be sure that you know how to make the different signals for both right and left turns.

Make a right turn with your left arm raised from the elbow. Make a left turn with your left arm straight out.

BIKE LIGHTS

If you must ride at night or in dim or fading daylight, be sure your bike is well lit!

In darkness you must have a front bike **light** that can be seen for at least 500 feet. You need a rear red **reflector** light that can be seen 600 feet away. You also need side reflectors on your bike's **spokes** and reflectors on your bike **pedals**. Wear white or reflective clothing at night, too.

AVOID SURPRISE PROBLEMS

You can reduce the chance of a surprise problem by not riding too fast for conditions. Hazards—things that are dangerous—are much easier to avoid if you have time to stop or swerve around them.

If you approach another biker or a person walking, pass on the left. Do not surprise them! Use your bell or horn, or speak to the person ahead. ●

Strategy Follow-up

On a separate sheet of paper, create a simple outline for the second part of this selection. Begin your outline with 4. *Rules of the Road*.

✓Personal Checklist

Read each question and put a check (✓) in the correct box.

1. How well were you able to use context to understand the specialized vocabulary in this selection?
   ☐ 3 (extremely well)
   ☐ 2 (fairly well)
   ☐ 1 (not well)

2. In the Vocabulary Builder, how well were you able to label the parts of a bicycle?
   ☐ 3 (extremely well)
   ☐ 2 (fairly well)
   ☐ 1 (not well)

3. How well were you able to complete an outline for the second part of this selection?
   ☐ 3 (extremely well)
   ☐ 2 (fairly well)
   ☐ 1 (not well)

4. How well do you understand the importance of bike safety?
   ☐ 3 (extremely well)
   ☐ 2 (fairly well)
   ☐ 1 (not well)

5. How well do you understand how to choose the right bike?
   ☐ 3 (extremely well)
   ☐ 2 (fairly well)
   ☐ 1 (not well)

Vocabulary Check

Look back at the work you did in the Vocabulary Builder. Then answer each question by circling the correct letter.

1. Which list contains four safety features?
   a. brakes, spokes, pedals, seat
   b. reflector, light, bell, horn
   c. handlebars, horn, tires, frame

2. According to this selection, where should you put reflectors on a bike?
   a. on the tires and the bell
   b. on the frame and the seat
   c. on the spokes and the pedals

3. Which definition of *light* fits the context of this selection?
   a. special understanding
   b. time of day
   c. object that helps one see

4. Which definition of *frame* fits the context of this selection?
   a. underlying support or skeleton
   b. square used to record a bowling score
   c. one picture in a filmstrip

5. Which two safety features make noise?
   a. the light and the bell
   b. the bell and the horn
   c. the reflector and the bell

Add the numbers that you just checked to get your Personal Checklist score. Fill in your score here. Then turn to page 203 and transfer your score onto Graph 1.

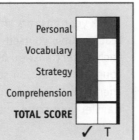

Check your answers with your teacher. Give yourself 1 point for each correct answer, and fill in your Vocabulary score here. Then turn to page 203 and transfer your score onto Graph 1.

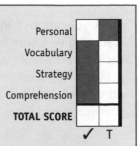

Strategy Check

Look back at the outline you completed for the Strategy Follow-up. Then answer these questions:

1. What did you write for main idea #8?
   a. Helmets
   b. Bike Lights
   c. Using Your Hands

2. Which supporting detail does *not* belong under Rules of the Road?
   a. Never ride with two people on a one-seat bike.
   b. Ride on the right, in the same direction as cars and trucks.
   c. Obey road signs and traffic signals.

3. Which supporting detail belongs under Bike Lights?
   a. You need a rear red reflector light that can be seen 600 feet away.
   b. If you approach another biker or a person walking, pass on the left.
   c. If you can't touch your feet to the ground while standing, the bike is too big.

4. Which section tells you about not riding too fast?
   a. Playing It Safe
   b. Using Your Hands
   c. Avoid Surprise Problems

5. How might you use this outline?
   a. to remember the parts of a bicycle
   b. to organize bicycle safety information
   c. to remember the history of bicycles

Comprehension Check

Review the selection if necessary. Then answer these questions:

1. Why is it important to know how to ride a bike safely?
   a. Riding safely can avoid accidents.
   b. Riding a bike can be dangerous.
   c. Both answers above are correct.

2. Why is it important to have a bike that fits you?
   a. The bike should match your personality.
   b. A good fit is important for safe riding.
   c. Both answers above are correct.

3. When are you considered part of traffic?
   a. when you ride a bike on the street
   b. when you ride a bike on the sidewalk
   c. when you ride a bike in the park

4. When are you allowed to have only one hand on the handlebars?
   a. never
   b. when making turns
   c. when riding slowly

5. Why should you wear white clothing when you ride your bike at night?
   a. to be seen
   b. to stay cool
   c. to stay clean

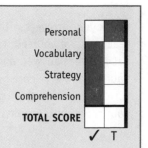

Check your answers with your teacher. Give yourself 1 point for each correct answer, and fill in your Strategy score here. Then turn to page 203 and transfer your score onto Graph 1.

Personal
Vocabulary
Strategy
Comprehension
TOTAL SCORE
✓ T

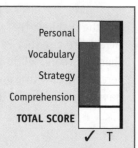

Check your answers with your teacher. Give yourself 1 point for each correct answer, and fill in your Comprehension score here. Then turn to page 203 and transfer your score onto Graph 1.

Personal
Vocabulary
Strategy
Comprehension
TOTAL SCORE
✓ T

Extending

Choose one or more of these activities:

HAVE A BIKE-SAFETY DAY

With your friends or classmates, set up a bike-safety day. Use your outlines from this selection, as well as any of the resources on this page, to help you create a bike-safety checklist. Don't forget to include ratings on your checklist, such as *poor, fair, good,* and *excellent.* Make several copies of the checklist and use it to rate both the bicycle and the rider. At the bottom of the checklist, write down anything that needs improvement. For example, you might write *Bike needs a bell and a light* or *Rider needs to learn the signals for right and left turns.* Give the completed checklist to the rider.

MAKE A POSTER OF BIKES AND SIZES

Find a bike catalog or visit a bike store to find out about the kinds and sizes of bikes that are available. Then make a poster that shows your findings. Cut out or photocopy pictures of the bikes and paste them onto your poster. Then write a brief description of the bike under each picture. Share the poster with your classmates. You might want to take a vote on the class's favorite bike or bikes.

TAKE YOUR MEASUREMENTS

Using the catalog or store from the activity above, find out how to measure yourself for the right-size bike. If you own a bike, measure it to find out if it's the right size. If you're thinking of buying a bike, take your measurement information to the store to be sure you buy the right size.

Resources

Books

Langley, Jim. *Bicycling Magazine's Complete Guide to Bicycle Maintenance and Repair for Road and Mountain Bikes.* Rodale Press, 1999.

Schwartz, David M. *Supergrandpa.* Lothrop Lee and Shepard, 1991.

Web Site

http://www.bhsi.org
This is the Web site for the Bicycle Helmet Safety Institute. It is a volunteer-staffed site, containing information on bike helmets and bike safety.

Greg LeMond

appendicitis

cyclist

defeat

gunshot wounds

internationally
famous

rescue helicopter

top form

willpower

Building Background

In this selection, you will read about a famous American bicycle racer named Greg LeMond. The selection describes his experiences in the Tour de France, the most famous bicycle race in the world. The map below shows the route of the 1989 Tour de France.

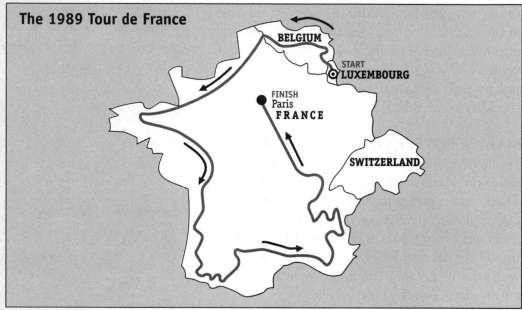

The 1989 Tour de France

CLIPBOARD
Difficult Time

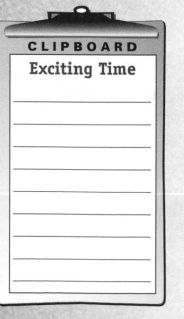

CLIPBOARD
Exciting Time

Vocabulary Builder

1. Before you read this selection, think about how each word or phrase in the margin might describe an exciting time or a difficult time in Greg LeMond's life. Then list each word or phrase on the appropriate clipboard.

2. As you read the selection, look for other words related to difficult and exciting times in LeMond's life. Add them to the clipboards.

3. Save your work. You will use it again in the Vocabulary Check.

Strategy Builder

How to Read a Biographical Sketch

- A **biography** is the story of a person's life, written by someone else. A **biographical sketch** is the story of a part of a person's life.

- Biographical sketches describe events in the order in which they happened. Therefore they are written in time order, or **sequence**.

- To make the sequence as clear as possible, writers often use **signal words**. Examples include *first, then,* and *a few days later*.

- The following paragraphs explain how Greg LeMond began cycling. Pay attention to the sequence of events as you read. Use the underlined signal words and phrases to help you.

> Greg had always loved sports that he could do on his own—hunting, backpacking, and freestyle skiing. <u>When he was 14</u>, he went to a camp for skiers. One of the best ways to stay in shape, he was told, was bicycle riding. And that's how it started. Greg and his dad, who was trying to lose a little weight, rode 20 miles every day.
>
>   <u>Soon</u> Greg entered races for 14- and 15-year-olds and won almost every one. He became almost unbeatable in the United States. But being number one in the U.S. didn't count for much. All the top cyclists raced in Europe. Could Greg beat *them*? <u>When he was 16</u>, Greg decided to find out. He entered the World Championship for Juniors—and finished ninth.

- If you wanted to show the sequence of events in the paragraphs above, you might use a **sequence chain** like this one:

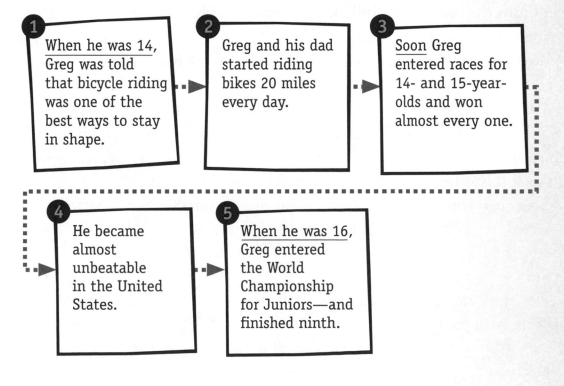

Greg LeMond

by Jim O'Connor

As your read the first part of this biographical sketch, apply the strategies that you just learned. Underline the signal words as you read. They will give you a more exact picture of when things happened.

The Tour de France is the most important bicycle race in the world. It travels about 2,500 miles around Europe over quiet country roads, twisting mountain passes, and busy city streets.

In Europe, bicycle racing is bigger than the Super Bowl is here. Bigger even than the World Series. And for three weeks each summer the race swings through France like a traveling circus and rock concert rolled into one. When the Tour ends in Paris, the winner is the world's number one **cyclist**.

In 1986, for the first time ever, an American won the Tour. He was a 24-year-old from Utah named Greg LeMond. Overnight Greg became **internationally famous**. And his future as a top racer seemed guaranteed.

The next winter Greg went to California to visit his family. On April 20, Greg went wild-turkey hunting with his uncle and his brother-in-law. The three men separated and moved through a field of berry bushes. Greg lost sight of the others. He stopped and then began to move again. Suddenly he was hit in the back with a full blast of buckshot. His brother-in-law had accidentally shot him.

Greg's uncle ran home and called 911. Then Greg had a stroke of luck. A **rescue helicopter** was flying nearby. It heard the police radio calls and flew Greg to a hospital with a center for **gunshot wounds**.

This quick trip probably saved Greg's life. He had 60 holes in his back from the one blast of buckshot and was bleeding from every one of them. If the trip had been any longer, he would have bled to death.

Greg spent the next six days in the hospital in terrible pain. Doctors removed most of the pellets. But two were in the lining of his heart. The doctors had to leave them there. Greg didn't know if he would ever race again.

"For three or four weeks," Greg recalled, "I'd sit at home in a chair, shaking with pain. I'd just cry and cry."

But little by little, Greg forced himself to take short walks. It was two weeks before he could go two blocks without tiring. Finally one day he climbed on his wife's bike and pedaled up and down the driveway. It wasn't the Tour de France—but Greg was riding again.

Soon Greg tried to bike a couple of miles each day. Then he took longer rides in the hills. But just as he was getting back to normal, Greg had more bad luck. He was rushed to the hospital with **appendicitis**. The doctors operated on him again.

That wiped out the 1987 season for Greg. He was sure he could come back to **top form** in 1988. But for the first time, Greg's **willpower** was not enough. By the '89 season, his ranking had dropped from #2 to #345!

 Stop here for the Strategy Break.

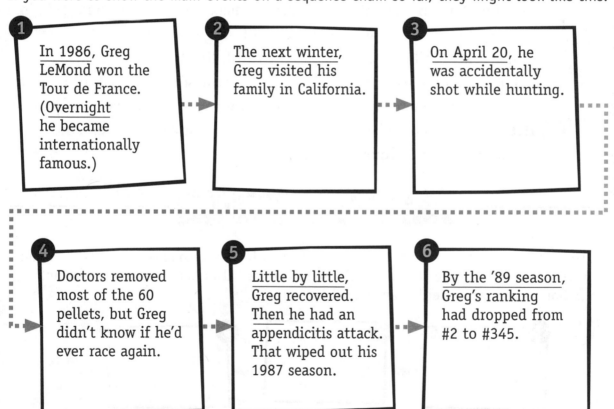

Strategy Break

If you were to show the main events on a sequence chain so far, they might look like this:

1 In 1986, Greg LeMond won the Tour de France. (Overnight he became internationally famous.)

2 The next winter, Greg visited his family in California.

3 On April 20, he was accidentally shot while hunting.

4 Doctors removed most of the 60 pellets, but Greg didn't know if he'd ever race again.

5 Little by little, Greg recovered. Then he had an appendicitis attack. That wiped out his 1987 season.

6 By the '89 season, Greg's ranking had dropped from #2 to #345.

As you continue reading, keep paying attention to the order of events and the signal words. At the end of this selection, you will create a sequence chain of your own.

 Go on reading.

People were saying that Greg LeMond was washed up. But he decided to race in the '89 Tour de France just the same.

In 1989, the Tour would be harder than ever. It would cover 2,025 miles in 22 days of racing. An extra day of mountain racing had been added, and there were three time trials—when the riders raced against the clock and not one another.

Laurent Fignon was a favorite. No one was betting on Greg—even he didn't expect much. His personal goal was to finish in the top 20.

He surprised himself by winning the first time trial. He began to think he had a chance after all. But Fignon kept pulling ahead. By the final day he had built up a 50-second lead.

The Tour finished with a time trial ending in Paris. Greg had only 15 miles in which to wipe out Fignon's lead. It would take a tremendous effort to win.

Greg decided to try a new kind of handlebars for this last leg. They extended out in front of his regular handlebars so that he could ride in a stretched-out, flat position that helped him go faster.

It worked! When Greg crossed the finish line he had shut out Fignon.

Greg won his second Tour de France by the slimmest margin in Tour history—only eight seconds! But he had won. After two years of pain and **defeat** he had come back to his place as the world's top racer. And in 1990, he won the Tour again! ●

Strategy Follow-up

On a separate sheet of paper, create a sequence chain for the second part of this selection. Begin with event #7 and go to the end of the selection. Fill in only the most important events. Don't forget to underline any signal words.

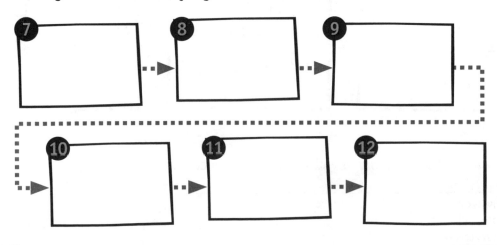

✓Personal Checklist

Read each question and put a check (✓) in the correct box.

1. How well were you able to use the map on page 134 to follow the Tour de France?
   - ☐ 3 (extremely well)
   - ☐ 2 (fairly well)
   - ☐ 1 (not well)

2. Before you read this selection, how many vocabulary words were you able to put on the appropriate clipboards?
   - ☐ 3 (6–8 words)
   - ☐ 2 (3–5 words)
   - ☐ 1 (0–2 words)

3. How well were you able to create a sequence chain for the second part of this selection?
   - ☐ 3 (extremely well)
   - ☐ 2 (fairly well)
   - ☐ 1 (not well)

4. How well do you understand how important the Tour de France is to bicycle racers?
   - ☐ 3 (extremely well)
   - ☐ 2 (fairly well)
   - ☐ 1 (not well)

5. How well were you able to understand why Greg's win in 1989 was such a great accomplishment?
   - ☐ 3 (extremely well)
   - ☐ 2 (fairly well)
   - ☐ 1 (not well)

Vocabulary Check

Look back at the work you did in the Vocabulary Builder. Then answer each question by circling the correct letter.

1. In 1986, what event made Greg LeMond internationally famous overnight?
   a. He was the first American to win the Tour de France.
   b. He was shot in the back while hunting for turkeys.
   c. His ranking as a cyclist dropped from #2 to #345.

2. Which word describes an exciting time in Greg's life?
   a. appendicitis
   b. defeat
   c. willpower

3. Which phrase describes a difficult time in Greg's life?
   a. gunshot wounds
   b. internationally famous
   c. top form

4. Which situation is an example of willpower?
   a. a rescue helicopter flying nearby
   b. racing again after a serious injury
   c. sitting in a chair and crying

5. Which situation describes Greg in top form?
   a. having appendicitis
   b. being shot in the back
   c. racing to a first-place finish

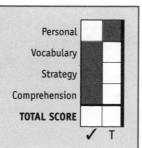

Add the numbers that you just checked to get your Personal Checklist score. Fill in your score here. Then turn to page 203 and transfer your score onto Graph 1.

Personal / Vocabulary / Strategy / Comprehension / TOTAL SCORE

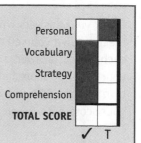

Check your answers with your teacher. Give yourself 1 point for each correct answer, and fill in your Vocabulary score here. Then turn to page 203 and transfer your score onto Graph 1.

Personal / Vocabulary / Strategy / Comprehension / TOTAL SCORE

Strategy Check

Look back at the sequence chain that you created in the Strategy Follow-up. Then answer these questions:

1. In the 1989 race, when was Laurent Fignon ahead by 50 seconds?
   a. after the first time trial
   b. after the second time trial
   c. by the final day of the race

2. When did Greg decide to try a new kind of handlebars?
   a. during the first time trial in 1989
   b. during the last leg of the 1989 race
   c. during the 1990 race

3. Which phrase is *not* an example of signal words?
   a. only eight seconds
   b. by the final day
   c. when Greg crossed the finish line

4. Which phrase tells when Greg regained his place as the world's top racer?
   a. by the final day of trials
   b. for the last leg of the race
   c. after two years of pain and defeat

5. Which sentence shows the correct order of events in this selection?
   a. Greg wins the first time trial, wins the '89 race, then wins the '90 race.
   b. Greg is ahead the last day, wins the first time trial, then wins the '90 race.
   c. Greg switches handlebars, wins the first time trial, then falls behind.

Comprehension Check

Review the selection if necessary. Then answer these questions:

1. How many miles does the Tour de France cover?
   a. about 25
   b. about 250
   c. about 2,500

2. What made the 1989 Tour de France harder than ever?
   a. An extra day of mountain racing had been added.
   b. There were three time trials.
   c. Both of the above answers are correct.

3. Who or what wiped out the 1987 season for Greg?
   a. a hunting accident
   b. appendicitis
   c. Laurent Fignon

4. Which of the following was a difficulty for Greg LeMond?
   a. gunshot wounds
   b. extended handlebars
   c. being an American

5. How many times does the selection say Greg LeMond has won the Tour de France?
   a. one time
   b. two times
   c. three times

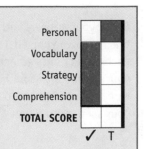

Check your answers with your teacher. Give yourself 1 point for each correct answer, and fill in your Strategy score here. Then turn to page 203 and transfer your score onto Graph 1.

Personal
Vocabulary
Strategy
Comprehension
TOTAL SCORE
✓ T

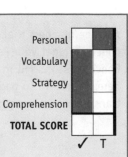

Check your answers with your teacher. Give yourself 1 point for each correct answer, and fill in your Comprehension score here. Then turn to page 203 and transfer your score onto Graph 1.

Personal
Vocabulary
Strategy
Comprehension
TOTAL SCORE
✓ T

Extending

Choose one or more of these activities:

RESEARCH THE TOUR DE FRANCE

Using the resources on this page or others, find out more about the Tour de France. Try to find such information as when it started, who started it, what route the first race covered, how many people usually compete, which countries have won, which country and/or person has won the most times, and how the race has changed over the years. Present your findings to the class in an oral or written report.

MAP THE ROUTE OF THE 1989 TOUR DE FRANCE

Follow these steps to map a three-dimensional route of the 1989 tour de France:

1. Find a good clear map of Luxembourg, Belgium, and France. Make sure the map includes physical features such as mountain ranges.
2. Trace the borders of the three countries onto a sturdy piece of cardboard.
3. Cover the borders with a layer of clay.
4. Look at the physical map to find the mountain ranges. Use more clay to make the mountains stand out.
5. Use the map on page 134 and brightly colored yarn or string to map the route of the 1989 Tour de France. Glue the yarn or string into place.

CONDUCT TIME TRIALS

Choose an activity that can be timed, such as outdoor running or walking races, completing a multiplication fact sheet, or building a tower of blocks. Using a stopwatch, set up time trials and have individual classmates race against the clock to complete their chosen activity. Record everyone's times, and post a ranking from shortest to longest times. (You can leave students' names off if you'd like.)

Resources

Books

Hautzig, David. *1,000 Miles in 12 Days: Pro Cyclists on Tour.* Orchard Books, 1995.

Lovett, Richard A. *The Essential Touring Cyclist: A Complete Guide for the Bicycle Traveler,* 2nd ed. International Marine/Ragged Mountain Press, 2000.

Porter, A. P. *Greg LeMond: Premier Cyclist.* Lerner Publications, 1990.

Web Sites

http://www.cnnsi.com/cycling/1998/tourdefrance/map
This 1998 Tour de France site features maps, race results, and information on the cities that the race passes through.

http://www.lvvelo.org
This is the Lehigh Valley Velodrome bicycle race site.

Video/ DVD

L. L. Bean Guide to Bicycle Touring. L. L. Bean, 1986.

Harriet Tubman

Building Background

From *Harriet Tubman* by Margo McLoone
Brave Conductor
Harriet Tubman helped hundreds of African Americans escape from slavery. A **slave** is a person who is owned by someone else. Harriet was a slave. She escaped to freedom and then helped others escape.

Harriet worked to stop slavery. She became part of the **underground railroad**. The underground railroad was a group of safe houses. Slaves who ran away traveled from house to house. Each home owner helped slaves escape to freedom in the North. Slavery was against the law in the northern United States.

The brave people who led the slaves north were known as **conductors**. Harriet was a famous conductor.

Civil War

conductors

Emancipation
  Proclamation

slave

track

underground
  railroad

Vocabulary Builder

1. Many of the words you will read in *Harriet Tubman* are explained in **context**. This means that the surrounding words and sentences contain examples or definitions that help explain the words.

2. The following sentences are taken from *Harriet Tubman*. Underline the context clues that help you understand the words in dark type.
   a. A **slave** is a person who is owned by someone else.
   b. The **underground railroad** was a group of safe houses.
   c. The brave people who led the slaves north were known as **conductors**.
   d. This kept bloodhounds from finding her scent. The dogs could not **track** her.
   e. In 1861, the **Civil War** began. A civil war is a conflict between people within the same country.
   f. In 1863, President Abraham Lincoln issued the **Emancipation Proclamation**. This written order freed all slaves in the United States.

3. Save your work. You will use it again in the Vocabulary Check.

Strategy Builder

How to Read a Biography

- In Lesson 14 you learned that a **biographical sketch** tells about a specific time in a real person's life. In this lesson you will learn that a **biography** tells about a real person's entire life.

- A biography is often written in time order, or **sequence**, from the person's birth until his or her death. To keep track of this sequence, writers often use **signal words**, such as *in 1860* or *when she was six years old.*

- The following paragraphs are from a biography of Abraham Lincoln. Notice the sequence of events as you read. Use the underlined signal words to help you.

> Abraham Lincoln was born <u>in 1809</u> in Kentucky. His family moved to Indiana <u>in 1816</u>, and his mother died <u>two years later</u>.
>
> <u>In 1830</u> the whole family moved to Illinois. There, Abraham worked as a clerk, a postmaster, and a county surveyor before going on to study law and grammar.
>
> <u>In 1842</u> Abraham married Mary Todd. <u>In 1860</u> he was elected President of the United States. <u>Three years later</u> he gave the Emancipation Proclamation, stating that all slaves would be free.
>
> Abraham Lincoln died <u>in 1865</u> after being shot while watching a play at Ford's Theater.

- If you wanted to show the sequence of events in these paragraphs, you could put them on a **time line** like this one:

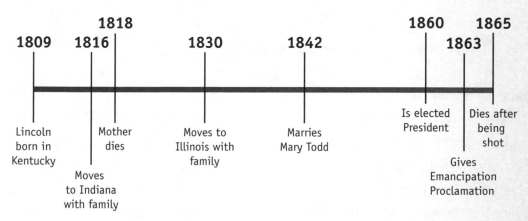

Harriet Tubman

by Margo McLoone

As you read this biography, note the underlined dates and important events in Harriet Tubman's life. (Be careful—one of the events is out of sequence.)

Young Slave

Harriet Tubman was <u>born in 1821</u> in Dorchester County, Maryland. She was one of 11 children in her family. Her parents were Harriet and Benjamin Ross. She was named Araminta, but her family called her Minty. <u>When she was 13</u>, she was given her adult name. Her adult name was Harriet.

Harriet started working <u>when she was six years old</u>. She worked in her owner's house. She dusted tables and scrubbed floors. She cared for a baby.

Harriet's owner was not kind to her. Harriet was often beaten. She slept on cold floors. She had very little food to eat.

<u>When she was seven years old</u>, Harriet tried to run away. After escaping, she became hungry and tired. She returned to her owner.

Escape Attempt

Harriet was not a good housekeeper. She was sent to work in the fields. The work was harder. But Harriet liked being outside.

One day <u>in 1833</u>, Harriet was picking cotton in a field. She saw a slave leave the field. She followed him to a nearby store.

The owner caught up with them. He told Harriet to help him catch the other slave. She refused. The owner threw a heavy weight at her head. It hit her forehead. She fell to the ground, nearly dead.

Harriet never fully healed. She had a deep scar. Throughout her life, she suffered from headaches and fainting spells.

Escape to Freedom

<u>In 1844</u>, Harriet married John Tubman. He had been a slave. But now he was free because his master had died. Harriet wanted her freedom, too. She knew African Americans were free in the North.

Harriet asked John to escape to the North with her. He said no. Harriet did not lose her dream. She said she would go free or die.

One night, Harriet left home in secret. She went to a trusted woman's house. The woman gave her directions to her next stop. Harriet would be safe at these places.

Harriet was hidden in a wagon and driven far away. Then she continued her journey. In 1849, she made it safely to the North. She was free.

 Stop here for the Strategy Break.

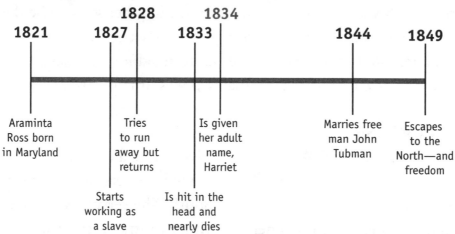

Strategy Break

If you were to show the most important events in Harriet Tubman's life so far, your time line might look like this:

| 1821 | 1827 | 1828 | 1833 | 1834 | 1844 | 1849 |

- **Araminta Ross born in Maryland** (1821)
- **Tries to run away but returns** (1827)
- **Starts working as a slave** (1828)
- **Is hit in the head and nearly dies** (1833)
- **Is given her adult name, Harriet** (1834)
- **Marries free man John Tubman** (1844)
- **Escapes to the North—and freedom** (1849)

As you continue reading, keep paying attention to the events in Harriet's life. Also keep looking for signal words, and see if any more events are out of sequence. At the end of this selection you will create a time line of your own.

 Go on reading.

Return

Harriet worked as a hotel maid in Philadelphia, Pennsylvania. She missed her family. She made plans to help them escape, too.

On Christmas Eve in 1850, Harriet returned to Maryland. She came for her three brothers and their families.

It was not safe to tell their parents the plan. Harriet's father, Ben, covered his eyes. He wanted to be able to tell his owner that he did not see anything.

Harriet safely led her brothers and their families north. She later returned for her most daring trip. In 1857, she took her aging parents north to freedom.

Bold Rescuer

From 1850 to 1860, Harriet made at least 15 trips to free slaves. It was very dangerous. By law, slaves who ran away to the North could be captured. Then, they were returned to their owners.

Slaves were not safe anywhere in the United States. People put up posters offering a reward for Harriet's capture. She started to lead slaves farther north to Canada.

Harriet hid herself in many ways. She moved through swamp water and rivers. This kept bloodhounds from finding her scent. The dogs could not **track** her. Harriet also carried a pistol for security.

Harriet led more than 300 slaves to freedom. She never lost one person. She was never caught. Her final trip was in late 1860.

Civil War Spy

In 1861, the **Civil War** began. A civil war is a conflict between people within the same country. Harriet joined soldiers fighting for the North. She fought against slavery in the South. She served as a nurse for wounded soldiers. She went into enemy territory to spy on troops.

Once, Harriet went on a rescue mission with Northern troops. They freed more than 750 slaves from prisons. Harriet served in the army for three years. People called her General Tubman.

In 1863, President Abraham Lincoln issued the **Emancipation Proclamation**. This written order freed all slaves in the United States. The war ended two years later. The northern states won.

Last Years

After the Civil War, Harriet brought her parents to New York. They lived in her house.

Harriet was free but poor. The army promised to pay her. Eventually she received payments of 20 dollars a month.

In 1869, Sarah Bradford wrote a book about Harriet. It was called *Scenes in the Life of Harriet Tubman*. Harriet earned money from the book's sales.

In 1869, Harriet married Nelson Davis. He was a Civil War soldier.

In 1908, Harriet opened a home in Auburn, New York. The home was for older African Americans. Harriet was 75 years old herself. But she continued to care for others.

Daring Woman

Harriet risked her life to help other people. She was not afraid of danger.

After slavery ended, Harriet continued her work. She fought for the rights of freed slaves. She worked to give women the right to vote. She built a home for poor and older African Americans. It was called the Harriet Tubman Home.

Harriet Tubman died in Auburn, New York, in 1913. She was nearly 93 years old. Today tourists still visit her home. It stands as a memory of the brave woman, Harriet Tubman. ●

Strategy Follow-up

Work on this activity with a partner or group of classmates. On a long piece of paper, copy the time line from the Strategy Break. Then add the following time line. Fill in the dates and information for 1850–1913. Some of the information has been filled in for you.

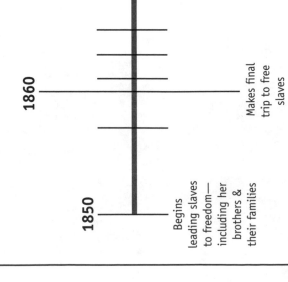

1850

Begins leading slaves to freedom— including her brothers & their families

1860

Makes final trip to free slaves

1913

✓Personal Checklist

Read each question and put a check (✓) in the correct box.

1. How well do you understand why Harriet Tubman was called a "brave conductor"?
   - ☐ 3 (extremely well)
   - ☐ 2 (fairly well)
   - ☐ 1 (not well)

2. How well were you able to underline the context clues in the Vocabulary Builder?
   - ☐ 3 (extremely well)
   - ☐ 2 (fairly well)
   - ☐ 1 (not well)

3. In the Strategy Follow-up, how well were you able to record the events in Harriet's life?
   - ☐ 3 (extremely well)
   - ☐ 2 (fairly well)
   - ☐ 1 (not well)

4. How well do you understand why Harriet returned many times to the South after she was already free?
   - ☐ 3 (extremely well)
   - ☐ 2 (fairly well)
   - ☐ 1 (not well)

5. How well were you able to understand why Harriet said she'd go free or die?
   - ☐ 3 (extremely well)
   - ☐ 2 (fairly well)
   - ☐ 1 (not well)

Vocabulary Check

Look back at the work you did in the Vocabulary Builder. Then complete each sentence by circling the correct letter.

1. In the context of this selection, what does *underground railroad* mean?
   a. railroad line built underneath the ground
   b. railroad that carried escaping slaves to freedom
   c. group of houses in which escaping slaves could hide

2. Harriet Tubman was a brave conductor. What does *conductor* mean in the context of this selection?
   a. person who directs an orchestra
   b. person who led slaves to freedom
   c. person in charge of a railroad train

3. Which meaning of the word *track* is used in this selection?
   a. rail that a train runs on
   b. path, trail, or road
   c. follow the trail or scent of

4. Which phrase means the same thing as *Emancipation Proclamation*?
   a. freedom statement
   b. slavery statement
   c. war cry

5. Who fought the Civil War?
   a. the United States and Russia
   b. the United States and Europe
   c. the northern United States and the southern United States

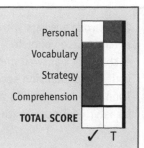

Add the numbers that you just checked to get your Personal Checklist score. Fill in your score here. Then turn to page 203 and transfer your score onto Graph 1.

Personal
Vocabulary
Strategy
Comprehension
TOTAL SCORE
✓ T

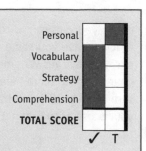

Check your answers with your teacher. Give yourself 1 point for each correct answer, and fill in your Vocabulary score here. Then turn to page 203 and transfer your score onto Graph 1.

Personal
Vocabulary
Strategy
Comprehension
TOTAL SCORE
✓ T

Strategy Check

Look back at the time line you created for this whole selection. Then answer these questions:

1. How much time passed between Harriet's escape to the North and the Emancipation Proclamation?
   a. about 12 years
   b. about 14 years
   c. about 16 years

2. Between what years did Harriet make trips to the North to free slaves?
   a. 1850 and 1860
   b. 1857 and 1860
   c. 1850 and 1865

3. How old was Harriet when Lincoln freed the slaves?
   a. about 13 years old
   b. about 42 years old
   c. about 44 years old

4. What two events happened in 1869?
   a. Harriet opened a home, and she got married.
   b. Harriet wrote a book, and she opened a home.
   c. Harriet had a book written about her, and she got married.

5. What did Harriet do in 1908?
   a. She returned to New York with her parents.
   b. She opened a home for older African Americans.
   c. She died in New York at the age of 92.

Comprehension Check

Review the selection if necessary. Then answer these questions:

1. How would you best describe Harriet Tubman?
   a. brave and caring
   b. sneaky and mean
   c. safe and sorry

2. What do you think might have caused Harriet to want her freedom so badly?
   a. Her owner treated her kindly and fed her very well.
   b. Her owner almost killed her when she was young.
   c. She was not a very good housekeeper.

3. Why do you think Harriet's trip to free her parents was her most daring trip?
   a. Her parents were older, so traveling would be harder for them.
   b. The Civil War was about to begin, and it was dangerous to travel.
   c. President Lincoln would soon write the Emancipation Proclamation.

4. Why did Harriet fight for the North in the Civil War?
   a. The South was against slavery.
   b. The North was for slavery.
   c. The North was against slavery.

5. Which of these causes would Harriet Tubman most likely fight for today?
   a. stopping people from wearing fur
   b. saving animals from extinction
   c. gaining equal rights for every person

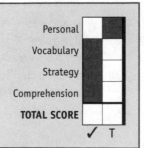

Check your answers with your teacher. Give yourself 1 point for each correct answer, and fill in your Strategy score here. Then turn to page 203 and transfer your score onto Graph 1.

Personal
Vocabulary
Strategy
Comprehension
TOTAL SCORE
✓ T

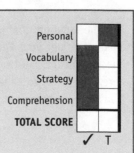

Check your answers with your teacher. Give yourself 1 point for each correct answer, and fill in your Comprehension score here. Then turn to page 203 and transfer your score onto Graph 1.

Personal
Vocabulary
Strategy
Comprehension
TOTAL SCORE
✓ T

Extending

Choose one or both of these activities:

WRITE IN CODE

Slaves on the underground railroad used code words to keep their owners from knowing what they were doing. Pretend you're Harriet Tubman, and you're trying to persuade your family to escape north with you. Choose Harriet's first husband, her brothers, or her parents. Then write what you would say to persuade them. You might write your words as a poem or a song containing code words that slave owners wouldn't understand.

INTERPRET A STATEMENT

"On my underground railroad I never ran my train off the track and I never lost a passenger."

The quote above is from the book *Scenes in the Life of Harriet Tubman*, written by Sarah Bradford in 1869. Write what you think Harriet Tubman meant when she made this statement. Share your response with a partner to see how your ideas are similar to or different from each other's.

Resources

Books

Bentley, Judith. *Harriet Tubman*. Franklin Watts, 1990.

Blal, Raymond. *The Underground Railroad*. Houghton Mifflin, 1995.

Ferris, Jeri. *Go Free or Die: A Story About Harriet*. Carolrhoda Creative Minds. First Avenue Editions, 1988.

Petry, Ann. *Harriet Tubman: Conductor on the Underground Railroad*. HarperTrophy, 1996.

Ringgold, Faith. *Aunt Harriet's Underground Railroad in the Sky*. Crown Publishers, 1992.

Web Sites

http://www.harriettubmanhome.org
This site shows Harriet Tubman's life in pictures and words and has links to related resources.

http://www.npca.org/walk.html
The National Parks Conservation Association provides a personal account of what it might have been like to follow the path to freedom.

Address

The Harriet Tubman Home, 180 South Street, Auburn, NY 13021

Learning New Words

VOCABULARY

From Lesson 13
• handlebars

From Lesson 14
• willpower

Compound Words

A compound word is made of two words put together. After his appendix operation, Greg LeMond didn't have enough willpower to compete in the 1988 cycling season. *Willpower* is made from the words *will* and *power* and means "power or strength of will."

Fill in each blank with a compound word by combining a word from Row 1 with a word from Row 2.

Row 1:   rain   pony   story   base   fruit

Row 2:   tail   book   cake   drop   ball

1. collection of fictional tales = _____

2. game played on a "diamond" = _____

3. hair pulled into a rubber band = _____

4. rich food made at Christmastime = _____

5. water that falls from the sky = _____

From Lesson 14
• cyclist

Suffixes

A suffix is a word part that is added to the end of a word. When you add a suffix, you often change the word's meaning and function. For example, the suffix *-ful* means "full of," so the word *thankful* changes from the verb *thank* to an adjective meaning "full of thanks."

-ist

The suffix *-ist* turns a noun that names a thing into a noun that means "a person who_____." In Lesson 14 you learned that Greg LeMond is a world-class *cyclist,* or person who rides in bicycle races.

Now write the word that describes each person below.

1. a person who plays the organ   _____

2. a person who takes a tour   _____

3. a person who draws cartoons   _____

4. a person who terrorizes others   _____

5. a person who creates art   _____

Multiple-Meaning Words

When you read "The Pudding Like a Night on the Sea," you learned that a single word can have more than one meaning. For example, the word *beat* can mean "defeat" or "mark time in music" or "mix with a spoon." To figure out which meaning of *beat* the author was using, you had to use context.

Now use context to figure out the correct meaning of each under-lined word. Circle the letter of the correct meaning.

1. The angry bull stabbed the bullfighter with its <u>horn</u>.

   a. musical instrument

   b. hard growth on the head

2. Jason found a <u>seat</u> in the front of the theater.

   a. thing to sit on, such as a chair or stool

   b. part of the body on which one sits

3. Julie found the <u>mate</u> to her red glove.

   a. one of a pair

   b. husband or wife

4. We <u>taped</u> our favorite TV show so we could watch it later.

   a. fastened with adhesive tape

   b. recorded on magnetic tape

5. I cracked the <u>bat</u> when I hit that last home run.

   a. wooden stick or club

   b. flying animal that comes out at night

VOCABULARY

From Lesson 11
- beat
- whip

From Lesson 12
- spark

From Lesson 13
- bell
- frame
- horn
- light
- seat

From Lesson 15
- captured
- conductors
- track

LESSON 16 The Drinking Gourd (Part 1)

Building Background

In Lesson 5 you learned that **historical fiction** is fiction set in a real time and place in history. Since historical fiction stories are made up, the characters in them may or may not have actually lived.

In Lesson 15 you read a nonfictional **biography**, or true account, of Harriet Tubman's life. Harriet was a real person who worked to free slaves through the underground railroad. The selection you will begin in this lesson is historical fiction about made-up characters who used the underground railroad.

Big Dipper

conductors

drinking gourd

farms

passengers

runaways

secret group

stations

Vocabulary Builder

1. The vocabulary words below are from Part 1 of *The Drinking Gourd.* Read the words in Column 1. They are all terms that people used when speaking about the underground railroad.

2. Draw a line from each underground-railroad term in Column 1 to its definition in Column 2. (If you're not sure of any of the terms, guess for now. Then come back and check or change your answers as you find the terms in *The Drinking Gourd.*)

3. Save your work. You will use it again in the Vocabulary Check.

COLUMN 1	COLUMN 2
passengers	Big Dipper
stations	runaways
drinking gourd	secret group
conductors	farms

Strategy Builder

Summarizing a Story

- Sometimes when you read a long story, it helps to stop once in a while and summarize what you've read. When you **summarize**, you briefly describe who is in the story, where it takes place, and what has happened so far.

- Summarizing helps you keep track of the most important details in a story. It also helps you predict what might happen next.

- Think back to the historical fiction story *Wagon Wheels* in Unit 5. Here is one student's summary of that story:

"The story **Wagon Wheels** takes place in the late 1800s. The Muldie family got free land through the Homestead Act, so they moved to Nicodemus, Kansas. Mrs. Muldie (Mama) died on the trip, so when Daddy and the boys arrived they built themselves a dugout and got ready for winter.

"Winter arrived, but the supply train didn't. The whole town ran out of food and firewood, and there was too much snow to go out and find more. Just as Daddy and the boys began to lose hope, some Osage Indians showed up. At first everyone was afraid, but the Indians left food and firewood and then rode away. The town threw a feast to celebrate, and Daddy told the boys to always remember how the Osage Indians saved their lives that day."

The Drinking Gourd (Part 1)

by F. N. Monjo

As you read Part 1 of The Drinking Gourd, think about how you might summarize this story. Note the main characters and the setting. Also note the most important events.

Chapter One

Fishing in Church

Tommy Fuller put his right hand in his pocket. There was his apple. Then he put his left hand in his other pocket. There was his ball of fishing line.

"Quit wiggling!" whispered his brother Sam.

"Sit up straight!" whispered his brother Andy.

It was late afternoon. The three boys were in church. They had been there all day long. Mother and Father were downstairs with Grandmother Dudley and the rest of the grown-ups.

All the children sat upstairs in the gallery. The girls were on one side. The boys were on the other.

Across the way Tommy saw his sisters—Helen, Kate, and Rachel. Tommy took a big bite of his apple. Then he took three more bites. Out of the window he could see a flock of geese pecking at the grass on the village green below.

"Let us sing Hymn Two Sixty-three," said the minister, Reverend Morse.

Everyone stood up. They sang

"Oh, God, our help in ages past,
Our hope for years to come . . ."

Tommy reached for his fishing line. He tied one end around the apple core.

"You'll be sorry!" said Andy.

Tommy opened the church window and threw out the apple core. Three geese waddled over to see what it could be. A goose picked on the apple core.

"Come *on*, goose!" said Tommy.

The second goose clamped the core tightly in her wide bill. Tommy tugged on the line. The goose rose up into the air.

"Got her!" said Tommy softly.

The goose squawked and fluttered. She would not let go. All the other geese hissed and squawked and cackled too. They made such a racket that the noise filled the church. Everybody stopped singing. Reverend Morse looked up at the gallery.

"Deacon Fuller," said Reverend Morse, "I'm afraid it's Thomas again."

Father stamped up into the gallery. "Thomas Dudley Fuller," he said, "turn that thing loose!"

Tommy dropped the line. The goose fluttered to the ground. Father led Tommy out of the church.

"You march straight home, sir," said Father, "and go to your room." Then he went back into the church and banged the door behind him.

Chapter Two

The Runaways

Tommy walked along, thinking of spankings. It was dark when he reached home. Tommy could see the evening star. He went to the barn to say hello to the horses. Father had named them Dan'l Webster and Henry Clay. Tommy gave them each an apple.

"*You* don't have to be good in church, do you?" Tommy said.

The horses stamped and snorted. Tommy saw the hay wagon piled high with hay. He wanted to jump from the hayloft down into all that hay in the wagon. So up he climbed, into the loft.

"Hi, Dan'l Webster! Hi, Henry Clay! Look at me!" he hollered.

Then he jumped into the hay wagon. Two hens squawked. Something in the dim loft said, "A-a-a-anh!" It sounded like a baby crying.

"Who's there?" said Tommy.

Dan'l Webster stamped his hoof. Tommy climbed back into the loft to see what had made the noise.

"Who's there?" Tommy hollered.

"Stop right there!" said a deep voice. "You won't take us alive!"

A black man stood up, covered with hay. He had an axe in his hand. Tommy was so frightened he fell back into the hay.

"Oh, my goodness, Vinnie," said the man. "It's only a little boy."

The man dropped the axe he held. "We just hiding," he said, smiling. "We won't hurt you."

"Does Father know you're here?" said Tommy. "What—what are you doing in our barn?"

"Is Deacon Fuller your daddy?"

Tommy nodded his head.

"He hid us here," said the man. A little boy stood up beside him. "That's my boy Little Jeff," said the man. "I'm *Big* Jeff. This is my wife Vinnie. And this is Baby Pearl. We running away!"

"Running away?" said Tommy.

"We going to Canada," said Vinnie.

"We up from Carolina," said Jeff. "We been following the **drinking gourd** every step of the way."

"The drinking gourd?" said Tommy. "What's that?"

"Shoot, boy!" said Little Jeff. "You mean you never heard of the drinking gourd? I'll show you." Little Jeff jumped down from the loft and ran to the barn door. Up in the wintry sky shone the stars. Little Jeff pointed to the **Big Dipper**, caught in the branches of an elm. *"That's* the drinking gourd!"

"No, that's the Big Dipper," said Tommy.

"Same thing!" said Little Jeff. "The front end of the drinking gourd points straight up to the North Star. Follow the North Star, and you get to Canada. Get to Canada, and you be free!"

"Thomas Dudley Fuller!" said Father from the shadows. "Didn't I tell you to wait in your room?"

"Father!" said Tommy, surprised. "I—I found Jeff and Vinnie and—"

"I see who you found. You found all my **passengers**," said Father. "Don't ask any questions. Help hitch up the horses. We've got to get started."

 Stop here for the Strategy Break.

Strategy Break

What has happened in this story so far? In the space below—and on another sheet of paper if necessary—write a brief summary of Chapters One and Two. Be sure to mention who is in the story (main characters only), the most important events, and where those events take place. When you have finished, use your summary to predict what might happen in Chapter Three.

Summary of Chapters One and Two:

_____

_____

_____

_____

_____

Go on reading to see what happens.

Chapter Three

On the Underground Railroad

Tommy and Father sat in the wagon. Jeff and Vinnie and Little Jeff and Baby Pearl were hidden in the hay. They were driving toward the river.

"I been a slave all my life, Tommy," said Jeff, sitting up in the hay, "until two weeks ago. That was the day I decided we would run away to Canada on the underground railroad."

"The underground railroad?" said Tommy.

"Shoot, boy!" said Little Jeff. "You never heard about *that* neither?"

"You see, Tommy," said Father, "the underground railroad isn't a *real* railroad with steam engines and tracks and cars. It's a **secret group** of people who believe slavery is wicked. They live in homes and **farms** like ours, stretching from here to Canada. Everybody in the group hides people like Jeff and Vinnie, helping them get away."

"And they got *stations* on the underground railroad," said Little Jeff.

"Like our barn!" said Tommy.

"And they got *conductors*," said Jeff.

"Like me!" said Father.

"And they got passengers!" said Vinnie.

"Like *us*!" said Little Jeff.

"They call it underground," said Father, "because it's a *secret*. Every bit of it *has* to be a secret!"

"You right," said Jeff. "We valuable property. My old master lost $2,500 when he lost us, if he lost a penny."

"Then I'm sure he'll send some men to try to catch you," said Father. "So you get back down under that hay."

"Nobody's going to catch me," said Jeff, "as long as I got my axe."

Then Jeff and Vinnie and Little Jeff and Baby Pearl all hid from sight.

REWARD

Ran away from his Master, Maynard Reeves Bond, of Larkspur Plantation on the Edisto River, Dorchester County, South Carolina, a black fellow about 30 years of age, named Jeff, 6 feet two inches high, wearing a brown wool jacket and denim breeches. Last seen hereabouts on October 15, 1851. Accompanying the runaway are his wife, Lavinia, age 28, and two children, Jeff, 9, and Pearl, 1. Whoever shall take up these four **runaways** and return them to their abovesaid Master shall have $250.00 reward. All Masters of Vessels and others are hereby cautioned against concealing or carrying off said Servants, on Penalty of the Law.

Charleston, S.C., Oct. 21, 1851.

"Tommy," said Father, "don't say a word to *anybody* about what happened tonight. Jeff's a brave man. I'd hate to see a brave man sent back into slavery. Promise?"

"I promise," said Tommy.

"Whoa, hosses," said Father. "This is the end of the line. I have to find the boat now. It's hidden here on the riverbank."

Father walked into the darkness. A whippoorwill called. ●

Strategy Follow-up

Did the events in Chapter Three turn out the way you predicted they might? Why or why not? In the space below, summarize what happened in Chapter Three. Then use your summary to predict what might happen in Part 2 of *The Drinking Gourd*. (You will read Part 2 in Lesson 17.)

Summary of Chapter Three:

_____

_____

_____

_____

_____

✓Personal Checklist

Read each question and put a check (✓) in the correct box.

1. How well do you understand the difference between historical fiction and nonfiction?
    - ☐ 3 (extremely well)
    - ☐ 2 (fairly well)
    - ☐ 1 (not well)

2. Before you read this story, how well were you able to match the underground-railroad terms with their definitions?
    - ☐ 3 (extremely well)
    - ☐ 2 (fairly well)
    - ☐ 1 (not well)

3. How well were you able to summarize what has happened in this story so far?
    - ☐ 3 (extremely well)
    - ☐ 2 (fairly well)
    - ☐ 1 (not well)

4. How well do you understand why Big Jeff and his family are hiding in the Fullers' barn?
    - ☐ 3 (extremely well)
    - ☐ 2 (fairly well)
    - ☐ 1 (not well)

5. How well do you understand why it is so important to keep the runaway family hidden?
    - ☐ 3 (extremely well)
    - ☐ 2 (fairly well)
    - ☐ 1 (not well)

Vocabulary Check

Look back at the work you did in the Vocabulary Builder. Then answer each question by circling the correct letter.

1. What is another name for the secret group of people who helped slaves escape to the North?
    a. passengers
    b. conductors
    c. runaways

2. When Deacon Fuller tells Tommy, "You found all my passengers," to whom is he referring?
    a. the runaway slaves
    b. the people waiting for a train
    c. the people helping the slaves

3. Which of these places would most likely be stations on the underground railroad?
    a. train stations
    b. farms
    c. churches

4. When Jeff shows Tommy the drinking gourd, to what does he point?
    a. all the farms in the area
    b. the train station near the farm
    c. the Big Dipper

5. Why do you think the people in this story use the words *passengers* and *stations* instead of *runaways* and *farms*?
    a. They want to confuse the readers.
    b. They are playing a word game.
    c. They are trying to keep their plans secret.

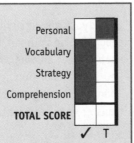

Add the numbers that you just checked to get your Personal Checklist score. Fill in your score here. Then turn to page 203 and transfer your score onto Graph 1.

Personal
Vocabulary
Strategy
Comprehension
TOTAL SCORE
✓ T

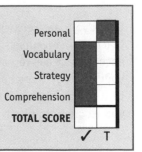

Check your answers with your teacher. Give yourself 1 point for each correct answer, and fill in your Vocabulary score here. Then turn to page 203 and transfer your score onto Graph 1.

Personal
Vocabulary
Strategy
Comprehension
TOTAL SCORE
✓ T

Strategy Check

Look back at the summaries you wrote for Part 1 of *The Drinking Gourd*. Then answer these questions:

1. Who are the main characters in Part 1 of *The Drinking Gourd*?
   a. Tommy Fuller, Deacon Fuller, and the runaway family
   b. Sam Fuller, Dan'l Webster, and Henry Clay
   c. Andy Fuller, Grandmother Dudley, and Reverend Morse

2. In which two main settings does Part 1 take place?
   a. a barn and a train station
   b. a church and Tommy's bedroom
   c. a church and a barn

3. What is a main event in Chapter One?
   a. Tommy eats an apple in church.
   b. Tommy sings Hymn Two Sixty-three.
   c. Tommy gets sent home from church.

4. What is a *not* a main event in Chapter Two?
   a. Tommy walks to the barn.
   b. Tommy gives each horse an apple.
   c. Tommy finds the runaway slaves.

5. Which sentence best summarizes Part 1 of *The Drinking Gourd*?
   a. Tommy hides Big Jeff's family and tries to find them.
   b. Tommy finds Big Jeff's family and tries to help hide them.
   c. Tommy finds Big Jeff's family and tries to hide from them.

Comprehension Check

Review the story if necessary. Then answer these questions:

1. What can you conclude about Tommy from his actions in Part 1?
   a. He enjoys going to church.
   b. He enjoys taking care of animals.
   c. He gets into trouble a lot.

2. What frightens Tommy in the barn?
   a. The horses stamp and snort at him.
   b. He hears a sound like a baby crying.
   c. Two hens squawk at him.

3. Why is Deacon Fuller angry when he finds Tommy in the barn?
   a. He had told Tommy to go straight to his room.
   b. He doesn't like Tommy playing in the barn.
   c. He doesn't like Tommy scaring the animals.

4. Why are Big Jeff and his family running away to Canada?
   a. They want to ride on an underground train.
   b. They don't want to be slaves anymore.
   c. They want to get to the drinking gourd.

5. Why is Deacon Fuller helping Big Jeff and his family escape?
   a. He belongs to the group of the people who believe slavery is wicked.
   b. He wants to capture the family and take the reward money.
   c. He doesn't like Big Jeff's master and wants to steal his slaves.

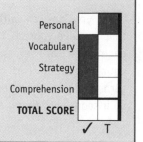

Check your answers with your teacher. Give yourself 1 point for each correct answer, and fill in your Strategy score here. Then turn to page 203 and transfer your score onto Graph 1.

Personal
Vocabulary
Strategy
Comprehension
TOTAL SCORE

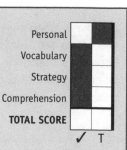

Check your answers with your teacher. Give yourself 1 point for each correct answer, and fill in your Comprehension score here. Then turn to page 203 and transfer your score onto Graph 1.

Personal
Vocabulary
Strategy
Comprehension
TOTAL SCORE

Extending

Choose one or both of these activities:

WRITE A SONG ABOUT THE DRINKING GOURD

As they traveled north to freedom, runaway slaves used to sing a song called "Follow the Drinking Gourd." Here is the first verse:

> Follow the drinking gourd,
> Follow the drinking gourd,
> For the old man is waiting
>   for to carry you to freedom
> If you follow the drinking gourd.

Using what you learned in this lesson, write another song about the drinking gourd. Before you get started, you might want to find all the words to "Follow the Drinking Gourd" for some ideas. You can find the words and music in *Gonna Sing My Head Off! American Folk Songs for Children*. (See the Resources section for a complete listing for this book.) You also can find the words to the song on one of the Web sites listed on this page.

FIND OUT ABOUT DANIEL WEBSTER AND HENRY CLAY

The horses in this story are named Dan'l Webster and Henry Clay. Do some research on these real-life men, and find out why Deacon Fuller would have named his horses after them. Then think about your own pets or pets you would like to have. What famous historical figures would you name them after, and why? Draw your pet or pets, and write their names at the top of the page. Share your picture with a partner, and explain why you gave your pet or pets their names.

Resources

Books

Krull, Kathleen, collector and arranger. *Gonna Sing My Head Off! American Folk Songs for Children*. Knopf, 1992.

Winter, Jeanette. *Follow the Drinking Gourd*. Knopf, 1992.

Web Sites

http://www.nationalgeographic.com/features/99/railroad/j1.html
Follow the path that some passengers took on the Underground Railroad.

http://www.okbu.edu/academics/natsci/planet/shows/gourd
This site includes the words to the drinking gourd song. It also includes definitions of potentially unfamiliar terms in the song.

Video/DVD

Underground Railroad, hosted by Alfre Woodard. A&E Home Video, 2003.

The Drinking Gourd (Part 2)

Building Background

From *The Drinking Gourd* (Part 1):

"Tommy," said Father, "don't say a word to *anybody* about what happened tonight. Jeff's a brave man. I'd hate to see a brave man sent back into slavery. Promise?"

"I promise," said Tommy.

"Whoa, hosses," said Father. "This is the end of the line. I have to find the boat now. It's hidden here on the riverbank."

Father walked into the darkness. A whippoorwill called.

Read on to find out whether the four passengers gain their **freedom**. Keep looking for the main events to help you summarize and predict.

freedom

law

marshal

property

reward

runaways

search

station

Vocabulary Builder

1. The words in the margin are from Lessons 16 and 17. By now you are familiar with most of these words.

2. Use what you already know and the clues provided to complete the crossword puzzle.

3. Save your work. You will use it again in the Vocabulary Check.

ACROSS
1 what slaves were considered by their owners
2 "passengers" on the underground railroad
3 federal officer in charge of finding runaway slaves
4 this declared that slaves were property
5 what runaway slaves were seeking in Canada

DOWN
6 another word for "find" or "seek"
7 what people were paid for returning runaway slaves
8 what a safe house was called on the underground railroad

Strategy Builder

Using Summaries to Make Predictions

In Lesson 16 you summarized what happened in Part 1 of *The Drinking Gourd.* **Summarizing** helped you keep track of what was happening in the story. It also helped you predict what might happen next.

Go back and reread your summaries of Part 1. Then use them to predict what might happen in Part 2. Don't worry if your predictions don't match what actually happens. You'll have chances to make new ones at the Strategy Breaks.

I predict that in Part 2 of *The Drinking Gourd,* _____

_____

_____

_____

_____

_____

_____

_____

_____

_____

The Drinking Gourd (Part 2)

by F. N. Monjo

As you read, be looking for clues to help you make predictions. Also keep looking for the main events that will help you summarize the story later.

Chapter Four

The Searching Party

Tommy heard hoofbeats on the road. He saw lanterns bobbing. Four men on horseback rode up to the wagon and stopped. The men got down from their horses.

"Say, young fellow," said the leader, "I'm a U.S. **marshal**. These are my men. We're going to **search** that wagon. We're looking for **runaways**."

"Runaways?" said Tommy.

"A Negro slave," said the marshal, "his wife, and two children. There's a **reward** for them. You wouldn't have them hidden in that wagon, would you, boy?"

Tommy's mouth was dry. "You won't find anything but *hay* in this wagon," he said.

"Mebbe we better search it anyway," said the marshal.

Tommy was scared. He thought about Little Jeff and the others hidden in the hay. If the marshal found them, he would send them back down South! They would have to be slaves! They would *never* be free!

 Stop here for the Strategy Break.

Strategy Break

1. Do any of your earlier predictions match what has happened so far?_____
   Why or Why not? _____

2. What do you predict will happen next?_____
   _____

3. Why do you think so?_____
   _____

4. What clues from the story helped you make your prediction? _____
   _____

Go on reading to see what happens.

"Marshal," said Tommy, "I guess I better tell you all about it. You see, I'm Tommy Fuller, and I'm running away myself."

"You Deacon Fuller's boy?" said the marshal.

"That's right," said Tommy.

"Pshaw!" said the marshal. "This is the boy made all that fuss in church this afternoon. Fishing for *geese*!" All the men laughed.

"Father was boiling mad," said Tommy. "He was going to give me a licking. So I ran away."

"We're chasing the wrong wagon, boys," said the marshal. "You better go home to your pa, Tommy, and take your licking."

"Yes, sir," said Tommy.

"And next time you go fishing," said the marshal, "tell your pa I want you to catch me two ducks and a nice fat turkey. That's an order."

All the men laughed. Then they rode away.

Chapter Five

Over the River

Father came out of the shadows. Jeff and Vinnie sat up in the hay. Jeff's axe was still in his hand.

"Tommy, you did just fine," said Father.

"I thought the marshal would find us sure enough this time," said Jeff.

Tommy was too scared to speak.

"Take the wagon back alone, Tommy," said Father. "We have to row across to the next **station**."

Little Jeff jumped into the boat. Jeff jumped in too. He helped Vinnie and Baby Pearl get settled. A whippoorwill called. Father started rowing away. Tommy heard the dip and splash of the oars in the water.

"Good-bye, Little Jeff," Tommy whispered.

"Good-bye," whispered Little Jeff.

"Good-bye," whispered Jeff and Vinnie.

Father rowed into the darkness, and then the boat was gone.

Chapter Six

The Lawbreakers

It was late when Tommy got home. Everyone was asleep but Mother. She gave Tommy some supper.

"Is Father all right?" said Mother.

Tommy told her what had happened. Then she sent him up to bed. But Tommy stayed awake, waiting for Father to come home. He heard the front door slam. Then Father came up to his room.

"Tommy," said Father, "I believe in obeying the **law**. But you and I *broke* the law tonight. The law says we were wrong to help Jeff and Vinnie get away."

"I know, Father," said Tommy. "But can't you *change* the law?"

"I've been trying," said Father. "We've been trying for years and years. Someday it *will* be changed. But right now the law says Jeff and Vinnie are another man's **property**—property same as a horse or a cow, property worth $2,500."

"But Jeff and Vinnie are *people*," said Tommy.

"Yes," said Father. "That's why I can't obey that law. That's why I hate it. It's *wrong*!" Then he kissed his son good night and closed the door.

Tommy lay in bed, thinking about Little Jeff and the others. "If they just get to Canada," he whispered, "they can be free. . . ."

Out of his window he could see the bright North Star. And pointing up to it, in the dark night sky, sparkled the drinking gourd. ●

Strategy Follow-up

First go back and look at the predictions you wrote in this lesson. Do any of them match what actually happened in this story? Why or why not?

Next, write a brief summary of Part 2 of *The Drinking Gourd*. Include only the most important characters, settings, and events.

_____

_____

_____

_____

_____

_____

_____

_____

_____

✓Personal Checklist

Read each question and put a check (✓) in the correct box.

1. How well were you able to predict what would happen in Part 2 of *The Drinking Gourd*?
   - ☐ 3 (extremely well)
   - ☐ 2 (fairly well)
   - ☐ 1 (not well)

2. How well were you able to complete the crossword puzzle in the Vocabulary Builder?
   - ☐ 3 (extremely well)
   - ☐ 2 (fairly well)
   - ☐ 1 (not well)

3. How well were you able to summarize Part 2 of *The Drinking Gourd*?
   - ☐ 3 (extremely well)
   - ☐ 2 (fairly well)
   - ☐ 1 (not well)

4. How well do you understand why Tommy lies to the U.S. marshal?
   - ☐ 3 (extremely well)
   - ☐ 2 (fairly well)
   - ☐ 1 (not well)

5. How well do you understand why Tommy's father breaks the law?
   - ☐ 3 (extremely well)
   - ☐ 2 (fairly well)
   - ☐ 1 (not well)

Vocabulary Check

Look back at the work you did in the Vocabulary Builder. Then answer each question by circling the correct letter.

1. What do U.S. marshals do to runaway slaves in this story?
   - a. hide them from their owners
   - b. free them from their owners
   - c. return them to their owners

2. What does the word *property* describe in this story?
   - a. areas of land
   - b. slaves bought or sold
   - c. items used in a play

3. Which sentence shows that Tommy and his father broke the law?
   - a. "I believe in obeying the law."
   - b. "The law says we were wrong to help Jeff and Vinnie."
   - c. "Jeff and Vinnie are *people*."

4. What reward was offered for the return of Jeff and his family?
   - a. $25
   - b. $250
   - c. $2,500

5. What did runaway slaves want more than anything else?
   - a. property
   - b. freedom
   - c. rewards

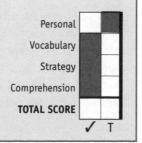

Add the numbers that you just checked to get your Personal Checklist score. Fill in your score here. Then turn to page 203 and transfer your score onto Graph 1.

Personal
Vocabulary
Strategy
Comprehension
TOTAL SCORE
✓ T

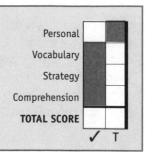

Check your answers with your teacher. Give yourself 1 point for each correct answer, and fill in your Vocabulary score here. Then turn to page 203 and transfer your score onto Graph 1.

Personal
Vocabulary
Strategy
Comprehension
TOTAL SCORE
✓ T

Strategy Check

Look back at your predictions and your summary of Part 2 of *The Drinking Gourd*. Then answer these questions:

1. At Strategy Break #1, which prediction would *not* have fit this story?
   a. The marshal will find the runaways in the wagon.
   b. The marshal will decide not to search the wagon.
   c. The marshal will find the runaways and let them go.

2. If you had predicted that Tommy would keep the marshal from searching the wagon, which clue in Part 1 would have best supported your prediction?
   a. Tommy's tendency to get into trouble
   b. Tommy's clever way of catching the goose
   c. Tommy's fear of getting into trouble

3. What is a main event in Chapter Four?
   a. Tommy gets stopped by the U.S. marshal.
   b. Tommy says good-bye to Big Jeff and his family.
   c. Tommy's mother gives him some supper.

4. What is the main setting in Chapter Five?
   a. Tommy's bedroom
   b. the river
   c. the wagon

5. What is a main event in Chapter Six?
   a. The marshal and his men laugh at Tommy.
   b. Tommy's father rows the slaves to the next station.
   c. Tommy and his father talk about breaking the law.

Comprehension Check

Review the story if necessary. Then answer these questions:

1. Why does the U.S. marshal stop the hay wagon?
   a. He is looking for Tommy.
   b. He is looking for Deacon Fuller.
   c. He is looking for runaway slaves.

2. Why is Tommy scared when the marshal stops him?
   a. He thinks he'll be punished for catching the goose.
   b. He's afraid for Jeff and Vinnie and their family.
   c. He's afraid the marshal will want to take his wagon.

3. Why does Tommy's father say, "Tommy, you did just fine"?
   a. He thinks Tommy could have done better.
   b. He is proud of the way Tommy lied.
   c. He is thankful that the slaves weren't found.

4. Why does Tommy's father disobey the law?
   a. He believes slaves are people and not property.
   b. He believes in breaking the law.
   c. He believes slaves are property and not people.

5. Why do you think runaway slaves usually traveled at night?
   a. There was less of a chance of being seen.
   b. They could follow the drinking gourd.
   c. Both answers above are correct.

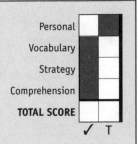

Check your answers with your teacher. Give yourself 1 point for each correct answer, and fill in your Strategy score here. Then turn to page 203 and transfer your score onto Graph 1.

Personal
Vocabulary
Strategy
Comprehension
TOTAL SCORE
✓ T

Check your answers with your teacher. Give yourself 1 point for each correct answer, and fill in your Comprehension score here. Then turn to page 203 and transfer your score onto Graph 1.

Personal
Vocabulary
Strategy
Comprehension
TOTAL SCORE
✓ T

Extending

Choose one or both of these activities:

WRITE A SEQUEL TO *THE DRINKING GOURD*

What do you predict will happen next to Big Jeff and his family? Write a sequel to *The Drinking Gourd* that describes their experiences. Before you begin writing, look back at your summaries for both parts of *The Drinking Gourd*. Use them to predict what will happen next, and then write your sequel.

FOLLOW THE PATH OF THE RUNAWAYS

Using the resources on this page or ones you find yourself, find maps of underground-railroad routes. Choose one of the routes and draw your own map of it. If you'd like, you can trace the route in yarn, string, or even silver stars to represent the drinking gourd. Hang your map on a bulletin board along with other classmates' maps. See how many different routes you can share.

Resources

Books

Brill, Marlene Targ. *Allen Jay and the Underground Railroad.* Carolrhoda Books, 1993.

Edwards, Pamela Duncan. *Barefoot: Escape on the Underground Railroad.* HarperCollins Juvenile Books, 1997.

Greenwood, Barbara. *The Last Safe House: A Story of the Underground Railroad.* Kids Can Press, 1998.

Web Sites

http://www.learnersonline.com/weekly/archive99/week5
This site provides a description of the Underground Railroad as well as personal stories, literature, music, maps, a bibliography, and links to related sites.

http://www.undergroundrailroad.org
This is the site of the National Underground Railroad Freedom Center in Cincinnati, Ohio.

LESSON 18 The Stars: Lights in the Night Sky

Building Background

What do you know about the stars? When you go outside at night, can you point out any constellations? Before you begin reading this selection, think of at least four things that you know about stars. Then think of four questions that you have about stars. As you read the selection, look for the answers to your questions.

astronomers

constellations

energy

galaxies

gases

light

Milky Way

universe

Vocabulary Builder

1. Use the words in the margin to complete the word map below.
2. Save your work. You will use it again in the Vocabulary Check.

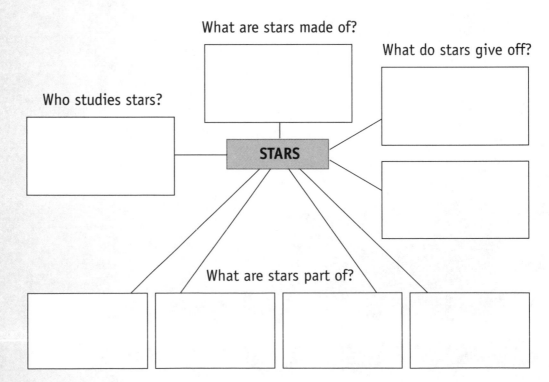

What are stars made of?

What do stars give off?

Who studies stars?

STARS

What are stars part of?

Strategy Builder

Summarizing Main Ideas in Nonfiction

- As you know, **nonfiction** is writing that gives facts and information about a particular subject, or **topic**.

- When you read a long chapter or a whole book on a topic, you're given much information at once. To keep the information straight—and to remember it better—it is helpful to stop often and summarize. When you **summarize** a section of text, you list or retell in your own words just the **main ideas**, or most important points.

- Read the following paragraphs from an article on the Big Dipper. Think about how you might summarize the main ideas.

> The Big Dipper is a group of stars that many people recognize when they look into the northern sky. It is part of a larger group of stars called Ursa Major, or the Great Bear.
>
> Some Native Americans consider the bowl of the Big Dipper to be a bear. They see the three stars in the handle as three warriors chasing the bear. Other people see the Big Dipper as everything from a cart to a plow to a bull's thigh—to the Chinese government!
>
> The Big Dipper had an important part in helping slaves escape to freedom. They sang songs about the Big Dipper, calling it the "drinking gourd." The slaves believed that if they followed the drinking gourd, they would find a better life. They used the drinking gourd's North Star to find their way to Canada.

- How would you summarize the paragraphs above in just a few sentences? Here is how one student did it:

The Big Dipper

- It's a group of stars found in Ursa Major (the Great Bear).

- People think it looks like different things.

- Slaves called it the "drinking gourd" and used its North Star to find their way to Canada.

The Stars: Lights in the Night Sky

by Jeanne Bendick

The Stars

What do you see when you look up at the night sky? You can see hundreds, maybe thousands, of stars out there. But that's only a few of all the stars there are. There may be more stars than there are drops of water in all the oceans on Earth.

You can see planets, too, in the night sky. We live on a planet—Planet Earth. Do you know how to tell planets from stars? Stars twinkle. Planets don't.

The stars look like tiny pinpoints of **light**. That's because they are so far away. Stars are very big.

One star looks much bigger to us than the other stars do, because it is much nearer. It's the star you see in the daytime. We call that star the Sun. Did you know that the Sun is a star?

What Are Stars?

Stars are made of burning **gases**. They are hotter than anything you can picture. They are hotter than firecrackers or furnaces. They are hotter than volcanoes.

Stars shine with **energy** they make themselves. The energy we can see that comes from our own star is called sunlight. We can also feel the Sun's energy as warmth.

The starlight you see at night is energy from those faraway stars.

Seeing Across Space

You don't actually see the stars themselves. They are too far away. What you see is the light each star gives off as it burns. The light has moved across space from the star to your eyes.

Distances in space are very big. The light from a star you see now may have left the star hundreds or thousands of years ago.

The light from another star might have left it when the dinosaurs lived on Earth. And yet another star may be so far away that its light began to travel across space before there were any animals at all. Stars this far away cannot usually be seen by themselves. We see them as part of a group of stars, their light all blended together.

Stop here for the Strategy Break.

Strategy Break

Did you stop and summarize as you read? If you did, see if your summaries match these:

The Stars
- There may be more stars than drops of water in all of Earth's oceans.
- Stars twinkle; planets don't.
- Stars look small because they're so far away, but they're really very big.
- Our Sun is a star we see in the daytime. It looks bigger because it's closer.

What Are Stars?
- Stars are made of very hot gases.
- Stars shine with their own energy.
- We see the Sun's energy as sunlight and feel it as warmth.
- Starlight is energy too.

Seeing Across Space
- We don't see the stars themselves. We see star<u>light</u> that moves across space.
- The light from some stars may have left them hundreds or thousands of years ago.
- Some faraway stars can only be seen as part of a group.

 Go on reading.

Where Do Stars Come From?

Stars are born. **Astronomers**—scientists who study the stars—think that it takes millions of years for a star to be born.

A star begins as a huge cloud of dust and gas. Slowly, the dust and gas come together until the matter is packed so tightly that it begins to heat up. It gets hotter and hotter. At last it begins to burn. The star is born.

Young stars are big and pale red-orange in color.

Do Stars Change?

As they get older, stars get smaller and hotter. They also change color. Some become yellow. Our Sun is a yellow star.

White stars are hotter. Blue stars are the hottest. Star colors tell astronomers how hot a star is.

Stars change over billions of years. They use up the fuel that kept them burning. When they start to cool, they spread out. The star swells like a balloon does when you blow it up. It becomes a red giant.

How Do Most Stars Die?

When its fuel is almost gone, a red giant falls in on itself. It shrinks and becomes a cold white dwarf, which is different from a hot white star.

At the end, it is a black dwarf star, with no heat and no light. Many stars die that way.

Pictures in the Sky

A long time ago, people gave names to the brightest stars. They also gave names to the groups of stars that seemed to stay together as they moved across the night sky. We call these star groups **constellations**.

The stars in constellations aren't really together at all. They only look that way. People saw in them pictures of imaginary beings, objects, and animals.

Crowds of Stars

Constellations are fun, but they aren't real. Some groups of stars, however, really do go together.

A great many stars travel together in clusters for as long as they live. Star clusters are like clouds of stars. A huge round ball of stars is called a globular cluster. The stars in an open cluster are farther apart, and the cloud has no real shape.

The Big Star Clusters

Really big star clusters are called **galaxies**. There are billions of stars in a galaxy. Galaxies have different shapes. Some galaxies are spirals, which look like pinwheels. Some are round. Some are shaped like footballs. Some have no shape at all that we can recognize.

Our own galaxy, the **Milky Way**, seems to be a big spiral with arms, rolling through space.

Our star and its planets and moons together are called the solar system. The solar system is out near the edge of the Milky Way galaxy.

Astronomers once thought that our galaxy was the whole **universe**. Now we know that there are even more galaxies than all the single stars you can see in the night sky. ●

Strategy Follow-up

First think about your questions from Building Background. Did you find their answers?
  Next, use a separate sheet of paper to write a summary for the parts of this selection called "Crowds of Stars" and "The Big Star Clusters." Be sure to list only the most important ideas, and skip unnecessary details.

✓Personal Checklist

Read each question and put a check (✓) in the correct box.

1. In Building Background, how well were you able to think of four things that you know about stars?
   - ☐ 3 (extremely well)
   - ☐ 2 (fairly well)
   - ☐ 1 (not well)

2. How well were you able to fill in the word map in the Vocabulary Builder?
   - ☐ 3 (extremely well)
   - ☐ 2 (fairly well)
   - ☐ 1 (not well)

3. How well were you able to write summaries for "Crowds of Stars" and "The Big Star Clusters"?
   - ☐ 3 (extremely well)
   - ☐ 2 (fairly well)
   - ☐ 1 (not well)

4. How well do you understand what a star is?
   - ☐ 3 (extremely well)
   - ☐ 2 (fairly well)
   - ☐ 1 (not well)

5. How well do you understand how a star is born?
   - ☐ 3 (extremely well)
   - ☐ 2 (fairly well)
   - ☐ 1 (not well)

Vocabulary Check

Look back at the work you did in the Vocabulary Builder. Then answer each question by circling the correct letter.

1. What are stars made of?
   a. very bright light
   b. very strong energy
   c. very hot gases

2. What do stars give off?
   a. energy and light
   b. galaxies and universes
   c. gases and constellations

3. Which of the following are stars *not* a part of?
   a. constellations
   b. astronomers
   c. the Milky Way

4. How are a galaxy and the universe related?
   a. A galaxy is part of the universe.
   b. The universe is part of a galaxy.
   c. A galaxy and the universe are the same.

5. Which of the following is largest?
   a. universe
   b. galaxy
   c. constellation

Add the numbers that you just checked to get your Personal Checklist score. Fill in your score here. Then turn to page 203 and transfer your score onto Graph 1.

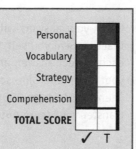

Check your answers with your teacher. Give yourself 1 point for each correct answer, and fill in your Vocabulary score here. Then turn to page 203 and transfer your score onto Graph 1.

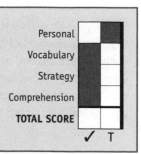

Strategy Check

Look back at the summaries you wrote for "Crowds of Stars" and "The Big Star Clusters." Then answer these questions:

1. Which of the following statements is true?
   a. Constellations are real star clusters.
   b. Constellations are not real star clusters.
   c. Star clusters are real constellations.

2. What are two kinds of star clusters?
   a. globular and open
   b. globular and round
   c. open and far apart

3. What are really big star clusters called?
   a. spirals
   b. galaxies
   c. round

4. To which galaxy does Earth belong?
   a. the solar system
   b. the Milky Way
   c. the universe

5. What makes up the solar system?
   a. all the stars in the universe
   b. all the stars in the Milky Way
   c. the Sun and its planets and moons

Comprehension Check

Review the selection if necessary. Then answer these questions:

1. How can you tell the difference between a planet and a star?
   a. Planets twinkle and stars don't.
   b. Stars twinkle brighter than planets.
   c. Stars twinkle and planets don't.

2. Why do stars look like tiny pinpoints of light?
   a. They are very far away.
   b. They are very small.
   c. They are very big.

3. From where does Earth get its light and warmth?
   a. clusters of stars
   b. the Milky Way
   c. the Sun

4. When is a star born?
   a. when one star breaks off from another star
   b. when a mass of dust and gas begins to burn
   c. when one star falls in on itself

5. What color are the hottest stars?
   a. blue
   b. yellow
   c. red

Check your answers with your teacher. Give yourself 1 point for each correct answer, and fill in your Strategy score here. Then turn to page 203 and transfer your score onto Graph 1.

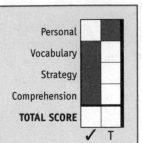

Check your answers with your teacher. Give yourself 1 point for each correct answer, and fill in your Comprehension score here. Then turn to page 203 and transfer your score onto Graph 1.

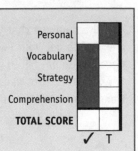

Extending

Choose one or both of these activities:

CHART STAR COLORS AND TEMPERATURES

Use an encyclopedia or a source listed on this page to find out more about star colors and temperatures. Turn your findings into a chart that you can explain to the class. Save your chart. You may use it again in science class.

DRAW YOUR SIGN

If there isn't a planetarium in your area, visit a Web site on the Internet that gives information about the stars. (Two are listed on this page.) Find the constellations for the signs of the zodiac, and draw the one that shows your sign. Draw an outline around the constellation to make it look like its name. Compare your drawing with those of your classmates. Which constellation looks most like its name?

Resources

Books

Branley, Franklyn Mansfield. *The Big Dipper.* HarperCollins Children's Books, 1991.

Dickinson, Terence. *Exploring the Night Sky: The Equinox Astronomy Guide for Beginners.* Firefly Books, 1988.

Moore, Patrick. *Comets and Shooting Stars.* Copper Beach Books, 1995.

Stott, Carole. *I Wonder Why Stars Twinkle and Other Questions About Space.* Kingfisher, 2003.

Web Sites

http://www.astro.wisc.edu/~dolan/constellations
This site gives information on constellations. It includes sky charts, photos, and names of stars and provides links to other sites.

http://www.mdsci.org/shows/davis/skycalendar/funfacts.cfm
Maryland Science Center's sky calendar describes astronomical events for every month and provides a helpful glossary.

The Fisherman Who Wanted a Knife

Building Background

From *The Fisherman Who Wanted a Knife*

Long, long ago, people did not use money. Instead, they traded with each other to get the things they needed.

What is trading? When you say "*I'll* give you my dump truck if *you* give me your kite"—that's trading.

When you say "*I'll* give you my candy if *you* give me your ice cream"—that's trading.

Long, long ago, before people used money, everybody traded different things. A fisherman traded the fish he caught for other things he needed. A baker traded his bread. A hatmaker traded her hats. A potter traded his pots.

money

Vocabulary Builder

1. The *Fisherman Who Wanted a Knife* is a story that explains why people use money. Before you begin reading, think about money and what it means to you. Record your ideas on the concept map on page 181.

2. As you read the story, add to your concept map any other categories or ideas that come to mind.

3. Save your work. You will use it again in the Vocabulary Check.

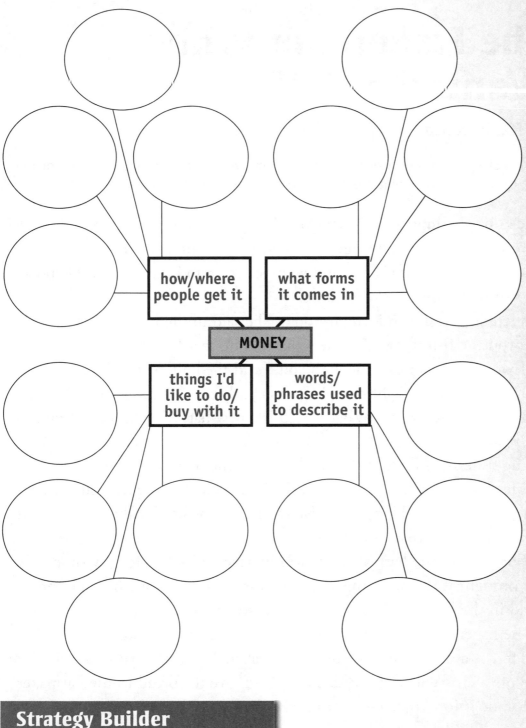

Strategy Builder

Identifying Problems and Solutions in Stories

- Throughout this book you've been learning that a main element of every story is its **plot**, or sequence of events. In most stories, the plot revolves around a **problem** that the main character or characters try to solve. Sometimes they try more than one **solution**. By the end, they usually come up with the solution that works—**the end result**.

- Think back to "The Hole in the Road" in Lesson 1. Review the problem-solution frame that you completed on page 12.

The Fisherman Who Wanted a Knife

by Marie Winn

In this story there are two different problems. As you begin reading, look for the first one. Notice the solutions tried and the result of each solution.

Once upon a time, long, long ago, a fisherman needed a sharp knife. Since there was no money long ago, he could not go out and buy one.

So he took one of his fish and wrapped it up to keep it fresh. He took the fish to the knifemaker's house.

"Here is a fresh fish I caught today," he said to the knifemaker. "I will give you the fish if you give me a sharp knife that I need."

"I would be glad to trade with you," said the knifemaker, "but this very morning a man brought me a large fish and traded it for a knife. Now I don't need another fish. What I need is a new hat. My old hat fell into the fire yesterday."

The fisherman took his fish and went to the hatmaker's house.

"Here is a fresh fish," he said to the hatmaker. "I will give you the fish if you give me a hat. Then I can give the hat to the knifemaker and trade it for a sharp knife that I need."

"Sorry," said the hatmaker. "I already have a nice fish for my supper. A boy brought it this morning and traded it for a cap. But I have no more bread in the house. What I need is a crusty loaf of bread."

The fisherman took his fish and went to the baker's house.

"Here is a fresh fish," he said to the baker. "I will give you the fish if you give me a crusty loaf of bread. Then I can give the bread to the hatmaker and trade it for a hat. Then I can take the hat to the knifemaker and trade it for a sharp knife that I need."

"I'm afraid I don't need any fish today," said the baker. "This morning my wife went fishing, just for fun, and she caught an enormous fish. But my best pot has a crack in it. What I need is a new pot."

Once more the fisherman went off with his fish. He went to the potter's house.

"Here is a fresh fish," he said to the potter. "I will give you the fish if you give me a pot. Then I can give the pot to the baker and trade it for a loaf of bread. Then I can take the bread to the hatmaker and trade it for a hat. And then I can give the hat to the knifemaker and trade it for a sharp knife that I need."

The potter looked at the fish. He sniffed it with his nose. He picked it up to feel how heavy it was.

"This is a good fish," he said. "It would make a delicious supper, fried over the fire. I will be happy to trade you a pot for this fine fish."

The fisherman gave the fish to the potter and traded it for a strong round pot.

The fisherman took the pot to the baker and traded it for a crusty loaf of bread.

Then the fisherman took the bread to the hatmaker and traded it for a soft leather hat.

At last the fisherman took the hat and went to the knifemaker's house.

He said to the knifemaker, "First I traded my fish for a pot. Then I traded the pot for a loaf of bread. Then I traded the bread for this hat. And now I would like to trade this hat for a sharp knife that I need."

The knifemaker took the hat and tried it on. It fit him very well and kept the sun out of his eyes. He picked out a knife he had made and gave it to the fisherman.

 Stop here for the Strategy Break.

Strategy Break

If you were to record the first problem, solutions, and end result on a problem-solution frame, they might look like this.

What is the first problem?
The fisherman needs a sharp knife.

Why is it a problem?
There is no money, so he can't go out and buy one.

Solutions to the first problem	Results of the first problem
1. The fisherman tries to trade a fish for a knife.	1. The knifemaker doesn't need a fish. He needs a new hat instead.
2. The fisherman tries to trade a fish for a hat so he can get a knife.	2. The hatmaker needs a loaf of bread.
3. The fisherman tries to trade a fish for bread so he can get a hat and a knife.	3. The baker needs a new pot.
4. The fisherman tries to trade a fish for a pot so he can get bread, a hat, and a knife.	4. **END RESULT:** The potter takes the fish for a pot. The baker takes the pot for bread. The hatmaker takes bread for a hat. The knifemaker takes the hat and gives the fisherman a sharp knife.

As you read the next part of this story, look for the second problem. Then look for what the characters do to solve it. At the end of the story, you will create a problem-solution frame for this problem.

Go on reading to see what happens.

"Here is my best, sharpest knife," said the knifemaker. "But what a lot of trouble you had getting this knife. You had to make so many trades. You had to go to so many people before you found someone who needed your fish!"

"Yes," said the fisherman, "everybody needs *something*, but it's not always a fish that they need."

"I have the same problem," said the knifemaker. "Sometimes I have to make many trades before I get the things I need. Sometimes trading takes so much time that I hardly have time left to make knives."

The fisherman thought very hard and then he had an idea.

"Wouldn't it be good if there were some easier way for us to get the things we need?" the fisherman asked. "Instead of everybody trading different things—fish and pots and bread and knives—wouldn't it be easier if people used one special thing for trading?"

"What kind of special thing could people use?" asked the knifemaker.

"It would have to be something really special, something you couldn't find just anywhere. Otherwise, people would not need to work to get it.

"It might be special, colored seashells, or little bits of gold or silver or copper. It might be almost anything, just so long as everyone used the same special thing," said the fisherman.

"That is a fine idea," said the knifemaker to the fisherman. "That is a great idea! We wouldn't have to do all that trading."

"If you gave me some pieces of that special thing, you could get a knife right away. You wouldn't have to make all those trades. I could give some pieces of the special thing to the hatmaker and get a hat right away. I wouldn't have to wait until someone needed a knife to get a hat," said the knifemaker.

"That's it!" said the fisherman. "Everyone would get some pieces of that special thing for the work they do—for the fish they catch or the bread they bake or the pots or knives they make. And then everyone would use those pieces of that special thing to get the things they need—food or clothes or tools."

The fisherman and the knifemaker talked to all the people who lived and worked in their village. They told them their idea.

"A great idea," everybody agreed. "Why didn't we think of it before?"

They picked small pieces of metal to be their special thing for trading.

Everybody used the same pieces of metal. And life was much easier and better for everyone.

Today too we use a special thing for getting what we need. Our special thing is also small pieces of metal—pennies, nickels and dimes, quarters and half-dollars. We also use specially decorated pieces of paper called dollars that we can trade anywhere for change—for pennies, nickels, dimes, quarters and half-dollars. We call that special thing **money**.

Money is not good for anything by itself. You can't eat it like bread. You can't wear it like a hat. You can't cook in it like a pot. But it makes it easier for us to get the things we need.

Today a fisherman still catches fish, just as a fisherman did long ago. But a fisherman today sells his fish for money. Then, if he needs a knife, he can use that money to buy a knife.

He doesn't have to trade his fish for a pot, the pot for a loaf of bread, the loaf of bread for a hat, and the hat for a knife, the way a fisherman had to do long, long ago, before people used money. ●

Strategy Follow-up

Now create a problem-solution frame for the second problem in this story. Don't forget to label the end result. Use another sheet of paper if you need more room.

What is the second problem?

Why is it a problem?

Solutions to the second problem   **Results of the second problem**

✓Personal Checklist

Read each question and put a check (✓) in the correct box.

1. How well were you able to understand the idea of trading in this story?
    ☐ 3   (extremely well)
    ☐ 2   (fairly well)
    ☐ 1   (not well)

2. How well do you understand why the fisherman had to keep trading in order to get a new knife?
    ☐ 3   (extremely well)
    ☐ 2   (fairly well)
    ☐ 1   (not well)

3. How well were you able to fill out the word map for the word *money*?
    ☐ 3   (extremely well)
    ☐ 2   (fairly well)
    ☐ 1   (not well)

4. How well were you able fill in a problem-solution frame for the second problem in this story?
    ☐ 3   (extremely well)
    ☐ 2   (fairly well)
    ☐ 1   (not well)

5. How well were you able to understand the problems people had before there was money?
    ☐ 3   (extremely well)
    ☐ 2   (fairly well)
    ☐ 1   (not well)

Vocabulary Check

Look back at the work you did in the Vocabulary Builder, and review this story if necessary. Then answer each question by circling the correct letter.

1. In which category on your word map would you put the words *dough*, *loot*, and *the root of all evil*?
    a. what forms it comes in
    b. things I'd like to do/buy with it
    c. words/phrases used to describe it

2. In which category would you put "from working at a job"?
    a. how/where people get it
    b. things I'd like to do/buy with it
    c. words/phrases used to describe it

3. In the United States, what forms does money come in?
    a. pennies, nickels, dimes, quarters
    b. dollar bills, checks, credit cards
    c. all of the above

4. Which of these do *not* describe forms of money in the United States?
    a. half-dollars and decorated pieces of paper
    b. metal and paper
    c. pots and loaves of bread

5. What *can't* you do with money?
    a. give it away
    b. eat it like bread
    c. get the things you need

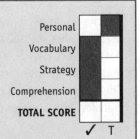

Add the numbers that you just checked to get your Personal Checklist score. Fill in your score here. Then turn to page 203 and transfer your score onto Graph 1.

Personal
Vocabulary
Strategy
Comprehension
TOTAL SCORE
✓ T

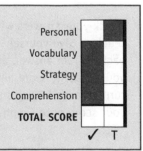

Check your answers with your teacher. Give yourself 1 point for each correct answer, and fill in your Vocabulary score here. Then turn to page 203 and transfer your score onto Graph 1.

Personal
Vocabulary
Strategy
Comprehension
TOTAL SCORE
✓ T

Strategy Check

Look back at the problem-solution frame that you completed in the Strategy Follow-up. Use it to answer these questions:

1. What is the second problem in this story?
   a. The fisherman can easily trade his fish for anything he needs.
   b. The fisherman uses one special thing to trade for what he needs.
   c. Everybody needs *something*, but it's not always a fish.

2. Why is this a problem for the fisherman?
   a. He has so many fish that they spoil before he can trade them.
   b. He keeps running out of fish, so he can't make trades.
   c. He has to make many trades before he gets the things he needs.

3. Why does the knifemaker help the fisherman?
   a. He and the fisherman have the same problem.
   b. He and the fisherman are best friends.
   c. He has no knives left and nothing to do.

4. What is one solution that the two men try?
   a. They sit around and tell each other how bad their problems are.
   b. They tell their idea to people who live and work in their village.
   c. They pick colored seashells to be their special thing for trading.

5. What is the end result?
   a. No one likes the men's idea, and they refuse to try it.
   b. Everyone begins trading seashells, and life gets easier.
   c. Everyone begins trading metal, and life gets easier.

Comprehension Check

Review the story if necessary. Then answer these questions:

1. In the beginning of the story, why did the knifemaker not take the fisherman's fish?
   a. Someone had traded him a fish that morning.
   b. His wife had caught a fish that morning.
   c. He really needed a loaf of bread instead.

2. What does *trade* mean in the context of this story?
   a. switch places with someone
   b. give one thing in exchange for another
   c. kind of work a person does

3. What did the people use as their special thing for trading?
   a. small pieces of metal
   b. small fish and knives
   c. small colored seashells

4. Why did the special thing have to be something that people couldn't find just anywhere?
   a. so they wouldn't be able to get it
   b. so they'd need to work to get it
   c. so they wouldn't need to work to get it

5. Which sentence best describes why people use money?
   a. Money makes it harder to get the things we need.
   b. Money makes it easier to get the things we need.
   c. Money keeps us from getting the things we need.

Check your answers with your teacher. Give yourself 1 point for each correct answer, and fill in your Strategy score here. Then turn to page 203 and transfer your score onto Graph 1.

	Personal
	Vocabulary
	Strategy
	Comprehension
	TOTAL SCORE

Check your answers with your teacher. Give yourself 1 point for each correct answer, and fill in your Comprehension score here. Then turn to page 203 and transfer your score onto Graph 1.

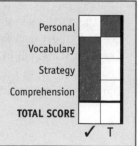

	Personal
	Vocabulary
	Strategy
	Comprehension
	TOTAL SCORE

✓ T

Extending

Choose one or more of these activities:

PLAN HOW TO GET AN OBJECT

Look through sale flyers or catalogs to find an object you'd like to have. Then think about how you might get it. Could you earn the money to buy it? If so, how? Would you be able to trade for it? If so, what might you trade? Try to think of fair trades or work that you could do in order to get the object you want.

TRACK A DAY IN THE LIFE OF "BILL"

Think about all the places that a dollar bill might go in one day. Then pretend you are "Bill" and write a story about your travels. Before you begin writing, you might want to track the places Bill goes on a sequence chain. If you can, role-play Bill's day with classmates who act as storekeepers and shoppers.

MAKE A MONEY CHART

Imagine you are going on a trip around the world. Find out what money is called in the following countries:

- France
- India
- Italy
- Japan
- Mexico
- Mongolia
- United Kingdom
- Zambia

Once you've learned the money's names, find out how much a U.S. dollar is worth in each country. (Use the resources listed on this page, or find others on your own.) Make a chart that shows what you find, and share it with the class.

Resources

Books

Adams, Barbara Johnston. *The Go-Around Dollar.* Simon & Schuster, 1992.

Bergen, Lara. *Funny Money.* Price Stern Sloan, 1999.

Berger, Melvin. *Round and Round the Money Goes: What Money Is and How We Use It.* Bt Bound, 1999.

Maestro, Betsy. *The Story of Money.* Houghton Mifflin, 1995.

Web Sites

http://www.pbs.org/newshour/on2/money.html
This site discusses the history of money, the stock market, and ways to pay for college.

http://www.x-rates.com/calculator.html
This site has a converter that shows the value of U.S. currency in the currencies of other countries.

All Kinds of Money

Building Background

In "All Kinds of Money" you will read about the history of money. Many people and places are mentioned. Do you know what people from Greece are called? What about people from the Yap Islands? Match the following groups of people with their appropriate country or continent. This will help you get ready to read "All Kinds of Money."

Africa	Chinese
Europe	Yapese
North America	Egyptians
China	North Americans
Egypt	Indians
Ireland	Greeks or Grecians
Greece	Europeans
India	Irish
Yap Islands	Africans

barter

credit

currency

metal

minting

receipt

wampum

Vocabulary Builder

1. Read the vocabulary words in the margin. If you do not know what any of the words mean, look them up in a dictionary.

2. Then circle the word or phrase in each row that is a synonym of the boldfaced vocabulary word. (Reminder: A synonym is a word that has the same meaning as another word.)

barter	trade	steal	borrow
credit	don't pay	pay now	pay later
currency	money	sell	buy
metal	shell	bronze	stone
minting	making gum	making mints	making coins
receipt	stone	animal	piece of paper
wampum	furs	beads	holes

3. Save your work. You will use it again in the Vocabulary Check.

Strategy Builder

Outlining Main Ideas and Supporting Details

- In Lesson 13 you made simple outlines to keep track of the main ideas and supporting details in *On Bicycles*. Making an **outline** is helpful for remembering important information. It is also helpful for studying for a test.

- Some outlines use a system of Roman numerals (I, II, III, IV, V, and so on) and capital letters (A, B, C, D, E, and so on).

- Read the following paragraphs, which tell why salt is important. Then read the outline of the paragraphs. Note how the main ideas are identified with Roman numerals, and the supporting details are shown with capital letters.

Salt

Salt is important for many reasons: It is a mineral we need in order to stay healthy. For thousands of years, we've used it to season food. And before refrigerators were invented, salt was used to preserve food.

In the first century A.D., Roman soldiers were paid in salt. Our word *salary* comes from *sal*, which means "salt" in Latin.

Salt

I. Important for many reasons
   A. Mineral needed for staying healthy
   B. Used for seasoning food
   C. Was used for preserving food
   D. Was used to pay Roman soldiers

All Kinds of Money

by Robert Young

As you read this selection, notice how it is organized. Think about how you might show the main ideas and supporting details in an outline.

Life Without Money

Live without money? How could you do it? It would be very hard today, but it wasn't thousands of years ago. The earliest humans had simple needs: food, clothing, and shelter. Small family groups could take care of these needs themselves.

But in time, as the number of people increased, so did the need for food and other goods. Family groups often traveled together to find things to eat. On their travels, they met other families. These groups began to trade with each other. This made it easier for people to get the things they wanted.

Let's Make a Deal!

When people began to farm, they grew more food than they needed. They traded the extra food for goods and services from people who had other kinds of jobs, like making clothing, making tools, and protecting the community. This type of trade is called **barter**.

Bartering is still used when people want to make a trade or a payment without using money. But barter doesn't always work. It is often hard to make a fair trade using things that are different. How much corn is a knife worth? What if you have something to trade that nobody wants?

The simple answer is to use money. Money is anything that has value, can be saved, and that people agree to trade with.

Early Money

Early money was often something people found useful. The early Greeks used oxen for money. People from Egypt and Crete used sheep. In England, during the times of Robin Hood, taxes were paid in horses.

Tools were very useful to people, so they were used as money too. Some African people used spearheads and knives as money. The Chinese used shovels. Early European settlers in North America used nails.

Salt has been another important form of money. That's right, the same kind of common salt we use in our saltshakers. But it wasn't always so common. Long ago salt was hard to get. Most of it was underground and had to be dug from deep within the earth.

Some early money was whatever people considered pretty. That's why shells were used as money in many parts of the world. People from China, India, and Africa used the cowrie shell. Iroquois Indians used pieces of whelk shells and quahog clamshells to make beads called **wampum**. These beads were woven into belts and necklaces and used as money. Colonists used wampum made by Native Americans too. In 1626 Peter Minuit, governor of New Netherland, used shells to help buy Manhattan Island. He paid Indians about $25 worth of shells, beads, and knives. Some people believe that this was the best buy in the history of real estate.

Some money was neither useful nor pretty. As late as the 1900s, people who lived on the Pacific islands of Yap used stones for their money. These weren't just any stones. The money was made from aragonite, a brownish white stone with large crystals like quartz. Since there was no aragonite on Yap, people paddled canoes hundreds of miles to another island, Palau, to get the stones. The Yapese worked the stones into round shapes and drilled holes in the middle of them. Then they put sturdy sticks through the holes so that more than one person could help carry the stones. Some of the stones were as big as 12 feet across and weighed more than a ton!

People have used many other things as money over the years. Soap, cocoa beans, and elephant-tail hairs have been used. Grain, animal skins, fishhooks, and feathers have also been used. So have tea, tobacco, bird claws, and bear teeth.

 Stop here for the Strategy Break.

Strategy Break

If you were to outline the main ideas and supporting details in this selection so far, your outline might look like this:

All Kinds of Money

Life Without Money
 I. Earliest humans didn't need money because their needs were simple.
 II. Needs began to increase, and families began to trade for what they needed.

Let's Make a Deal!
 I. People began to barter their extra supplies for goods and services.
 II. Bartering is still used, but it doesn't always work—it's hard to make a fair trade using things that are different.

Early Money
 I. Some early money was what people found useful.
   A. Greeks used oxen.
   B. Egypt and Crete used sheep.
   C. English used horses.
   D. Some Africans used spearheads and knives.
   E. Chinese used shovels.
   F. European settlers in North America used nails.
   G. Some people used salt.
 II. Some early money was what people considered pretty.
   A. China, India, and Africa used cowrie shells.
   B. Iroquois Indians used belts and necklaces made of wampum.
 III. Some money was neither useful nor pretty.
   A. Yapese used aragonite stones—some 12 feet across and weighing more than a ton!
 IV. People have used many other things as money over the years.
   A. Soap, cocoa beans, and elephant hairs have been used.
   B. Grain, animal skins, fishhooks, and feathers have also been used.
   C. So have tea, tobacco, bird claws, and bear teeth.

As you continue reading, keep paying attention to the main ideas and supporting details. At the end of this selection, you will use some of them to complete an outline of your own.

 Go on reading to see what happens.

Problems with Money

Why aren't these things used for money anymore? Why don't we carry bird claws or salt or shells to the store with us when we want to buy something? The reason is that there were problems with most types of money.

Some money, like grain and beans, spoiled. Other money, like shells and tools and feathers, got smashed or broken. Big rocks and oxen were too big to carry around. Salt was ruined easily. How do you make change when you use sheep or horses for money? And what happens when your money dies?

Money made from **metal** was different. It didn't spoil, ruin, or break easily. It couldn't die. And it was easy to use. That's why people have been using metal money for almost five thousand years.

At first people used any size or shape of metal. Since precious metals were used, the weight was important. The heavier the piece, the more it was worth. That meant that the pieces of metal had to be weighed. Imagine having your money weighed anytime you wanted to buy something!

Weighing money was a lot of trouble. So some people began marking the metal to show its weight. By marking the metal, they were **minting**, or producing, the first coins. But there was a problem. People did not all weigh and mark the metal the same way. Some people had bad equipment; others were dishonest.

There were other problems with making coins out of valuable metals like gold and silver. When a person needed change, very small coins had to be made. Some ancient coins are so tiny you could put them through an eyelet of your shoe!

The First Coins, Bills, & Credit

Around 700 B.C. in Lydia, a small country in what is now Turkey, the king decided that only his men could make coins. Lydia became the first country to make coins. This was the first known **currency**, or money produced by and used in a particular country. Coins from Lydia were different from our coins. They were made of silver and gold. They were oval and looked like small buttons. An emblem, such as a lion's or bull's head, was stamped onto one side.

Around 600 B.C., the first Greeks began minting money. They were the first to put designs on both sides of coins. Along with pictures of animals, the Greeks also put the figure of the goddess Athena on coins.

The Romans minted coins beginning around 300 B.C. Their first coins were made of bronze. The largest and heaviest was called an *as*. One hundred of these coins could buy one cow!

Imagine trying to walk around when your pockets are filled with heavy coins. Not very easy, right? Luckily, there is paper money. It makes life easier whenever a lot of money is going to be used.

The Chinese invented printing in 50 B.C. One hundred and fifty years later, they invented paper. But it wasn't until A.D. 650 that they started printing paper money. Paper money was used more and more often throughout the world as trade between countries grew.

It wasn't until the 1600s, however, that paper money was used in Europe—and then only thanks to robbers. That's right, robbers! It was not easy to carry lots of coins a long way to buy things. It wasn't safe either, because there were so many robbers. Instead of risking having coins stolen, a person would take them to a goldsmith, a worker who dealt in gold. The goldsmith would give the person a **receipt**. The person could then use the receipt to buy something or to get the coins back.

Sometimes a person would write a note to the goldsmith. The note would direct the goldsmith to pay a certain amount of money to the holder of the note. These notes became the first checks.

There were no credit cards long ago, but there was **credit**, the system of allowing a person to pay for goods or services at a later date. In Europe during the Middle Ages, knights did not want to carry cash around because of robbers. Instead, knights wore special rings. When a knight stayed at an inn, he stamped the bill with his ring. The innkeeper later took the stamped bill to the knight's castle to be paid.

We don't use special rings to charge things anymore. We don't use notes or receipts from goldsmiths either. And we certainly don't use cocoa beans, fishhooks, or bear teeth to buy things.

One thing is for sure: money is much easier to use today! ●

Strategy Follow-up

Work with a group of classmates to complete this activity. First, review the second part of "All Kinds of Money." Then, on a separate sheet of paper, create an outline for "Problems with Money" and "The First Coins, Bills, & Credit." Be sure to include only the most important ideas, and skip unnecessary details. If you can, compare your outline with those of other groups. See if your outlines all contain similar information.

✓Personal Checklist

Read each question and put a check (✓) in the correct box.

1. In Building Background, how well were you able to match the groups of people with their appropriate country or continent?
   - ☐ 3 (extremely well)
   - ☐ 2 (fairly well)
   - ☐ 1 (not well)

2. In the Vocabulary Builder, how well were you able circle synonyms of the boldfaced words?
   - ☐ 3 (extremely well)
   - ☐ 2 (fairly well)
   - ☐ 1 (not well)

3. How well were you able to help your group outline the second part of this selection?
   - ☐ 3 (extremely well)
   - ☐ 2 (fairly well)
   - ☐ 1 (not well)

4. How well do you understand why bartering doesn't always work?
   - ☐ 3 (extremely well)
   - ☐ 2 (fairly well)
   - ☐ 1 (not well)

5. How well were you able to understand why money is now made out of metal and paper?
   - ☐ 3 (extremely well)
   - ☐ 2 (fairly well)
   - ☐ 1 (not well)

Vocabulary Check

Look back at the work you did in the Vocabulary Builder. Then answer each question by circling the correct letter.

1. Which item would a person be most likely to buy on credit?
   - a. a pack of gum
   - b. a pair of pants
   - c. a refrigerator

2. How is currency used?
   - a. to buy and sell things
   - b. to give receipts
   - c. to lend things on credit

3. Why do we use money made of metal?
   - a. It doesn't spoil or break.
   - b. It wears out quite easily.
   - c. It is expensive to make.

4. In the 1600s, why did people start using receipts?
   - a. to be able to return what they bought
   - b. to avoid the risk of being robbed
   - c. to be able to barter more easily

5. What was wampum made from?
   - a. aragonite
   - b. shells
   - c. stones

Add the numbers that you just checked to get your Personal Checklist score. Fill in your score here. Then turn to page 203 and transfer your score onto Graph 1.

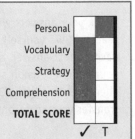

Check your answers with your teacher. Give yourself 1 point for each correct answer, and fill in your Vocabulary score here. Then turn to page 203 and transfer your score onto Graph 1.

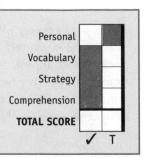

Strategy Check

Look back at the outline that your group completed in the Strategy Follow-up. Use it to answer these questions:

1. What would *not* be a supporting detail under "Problems with Money"?
   a. It got smashed or broken.
   b. It was easy to use.
   c. It was too big to carry.

2. Which detail describes how the value of metal money was first determined?
   a. The shinier the piece, the more it was worth.
   b. The larger the piece, the more it was worth.
   c. The heavier the piece, the more it was worth.

3. In which section of your outline would you include information about minting?
   a. "Early Money"
   b. "Problems with Money"
   c. "The First Coins, Bills, & Credit"

4. Which detail can be found in "The First Coins, Bills, & Credit"?
   a. Lydia became the first country to make coins.
   b. This type of trade is called barter.
   c. The early Greeks used oxen for money.

5. Which detail tells how credit worked during the Middle Ages?
   a. Knights stamped bills with special rings.
   b. Goldsmiths gave robbers receipts.
   c. Knights wrote special notes for people.

Comprehension Check

Review the selection if necessary. Then answer these questions:

1. Why did the earliest humans not need money?
   a. They never left the cave.
   b. They didn't know how to count.
   c. Their needs were very simple.

2. Why doesn't bartering always work?
   a. It's hard to make a fair trade using things that are different.
   b. It's hard to make an unfair trade using things that are different.
   c. You can only trade something that nobody wants.

3. Who printed the first paper money?
   a. the Greeks
   b. the Chinese
   c. the Romans

4. Which people were responsible for the use of paper money in Europe?
   a. robbers
   b. goldsmiths
   c. knights

5. What is good about money today?
   a. It's much easier to use.
   b. It comes in only one form.
   c. It's the same in all countries.

Check your answers with your teacher. Give yourself 1 point for each correct answer, and fill in your Strategy score here. Then turn to page 203 and transfer your score onto Graph 1.

Personal
Vocabulary
Strategy
Comprehension
TOTAL SCORE
✓ T

Check your answers with your teacher. Give yourself 1 point for each correct answer, and fill in your Comprehension score here. Then turn to page 203 and transfer your score onto Graph 1.

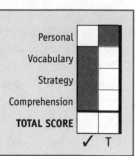

Personal
Vocabulary
Strategy
Comprehension
TOTAL SCORE
✓ T

Extending

Choose one or more of these activities:

DESIGN YOUR OWN "FUNNY MONEY"

Look at money from different countries, and think about why the symbols are so important to those countries. Then think about symbols that are important to your school or your classroom. Design some money to print or mint. Create one page of paper money and coins to photocopy and cut out. Trace existing bills and coins for sizes and shapes, or create your own. Ask your teacher to provide a "Funny Money" week to allow students to earn funny money for class rewards, such as extra recess or computer time.

FIND OUT HOW MONEY IS MADE

Using sources listed on this page or ones you find yourself, research how money is made in the United States. Draw a large sequence chain to help you keep track of the process. Then use your sequence chain to explain the process to others.

OUTLINE A MAGAZINE ARTICLE

First choose a topic that you are interested in learning more about. Then find a magazine article on the topic, and outline it to help you remember the information. Challenge yourself by outlining more than one magazine article. For a *real* challenge, combine the information into one outline!

Resources

Books

Barabas, Kathy. *Let's Find Out About Money.* Bt Bound, 1999.

Burns, Peggy. *Money. Stepping Through History.* Thomson Learning, 1995.

Rocklin, Joanne. *The Case of the Shrunken Allowance.* Cartwheel Books, 1999.

Video/DVD

Growing Up Well—Piggy Banks to Money Markets: A Kid's Video Guide to Dollars and Sense. Inspired Corporation, 2002.

Game

Moneywise Kids by Aristoplay.
This game helps kids learn how to accumulate, budget, and exchange money.

Learning New Words

VOCABULARY

From Lesson 20
- barter/trade
- currency/
  money
- wampum/
  beads

Synonyms

A synonym is a word that means the same thing as another word. In "All Kinds of Money," author Robert Young uses several synonyms for the word *money*. Two examples are *currency* and *wampum*.

Draw a line from each word in Column 1 to its synonym in Column 2.

COLUMN 1	COLUMN 2
search	delicious
right	correct
tasty	enlarge
difficult	fast
expand	hard
quick	look for

From Lesson 16
- conductor

Suffixes

A suffix is a word part that is added to the end of a word. When you add a suffix, you often change the word's meaning and function. For example, the suffix *-ful* means "full of," so the word *joyful* changes from the noun *joy* to an adjective meaning "full of joy."

-or

The suffix *-or* turns a verb into a noun that means "a person who _____." In *The Drinking Gourd,* you learned that Harriet Tubman was called a "brave conductor." A *conductor* is "a person who conducts, leads, or manages." Harriet Tubman led many slaves to freedom. Other kinds of conductors lead orchestras or manage railroad trains.

Write the word that describes each person below.

1. a person who acts _____

2. a person who edits books _____

3. a person who governs others _____

4. a person who creates _____

Multiple-Meaning Words

VOCABULARY

By now you know that a single word can have more than one meaning. When you read *The Stars: Lights in the Night Sky*, for example, you learned that the word *energy* can mean "heat" or "light" or "force." To figure out which meaning of *energy* the author was using, you had to use context.

From Lesson 16
- conductor

Now use context to figure out the correct meaning of each underlined word. Circle the letter of the correct meaning.

From Lesson 17
- property
- station

1. The box was so <u>light</u> that I carried it by myself.

   a. not heavy

   b. not dark

From Lesson 18
- energy
- light

2. Jan sent a <u>letter</u> to her sister in Florida.

   a. symbol of the alphabet

   b. printed message

From Lesson 20
- credit

3. You deserve a lot of <u>credit</u> for doing a good job.

   a. money in an account

   b. praise or recognition

4. How many <u>stars</u> are in the Big Dipper?

   a. balls of hot gas in the sky

   b. well-known actors or singers

5. Kim shook my <u>hand</u> when we met last night.

   a. part of the arm below the wrist

   b. part of a clock that shows the time

Graphing Your Progress

The graphs on page 203 will help you track your progress as you work through this book. Follow these directions to fill in the graphs:

Graph 1

1. Start by looking across the top of the graph for the number of the lesson you just finished.

2. In the first column for that lesson, write your Personal Checklist score in both the top and bottom boxes. (Notice the places where *13* is filled in on the sample.)

3. In the second column for that lesson, fill in your scores for the Vocabulary, Strategy, and Comprehension Checks.

4. Add the three scores, and write their total in the box above the letter *T*. (The *T* stands for "Total." The ✓ stands for "Personal Checklist.")

5. Compare your scores. Does your Personal Checklist score match or come close to your total scores for that lesson? Why or why not?

Graph 2

1. Again, start by looking across the top of the graph for the number of the lesson you just finished.

2. In the first column for that lesson, shade the number of squares that match your Personal Checklist score.

3. In the second column for that lesson, shade the number of squares that match your total score.

4. As you fill in this graph, you will be able to check your progress across the book. You'll be able to see your strengths and areas of improvement. You'll also be able to see areas where you might need a little extra help. You and your teacher can discuss ways to work on those areas.

Graph 1

For each lesson, enter the scores from your Personal Checklist and your Vocabulary, Strategy, and Comprehension Checks. Total your scores and then compare them. Does your Personal Checklist score match or come close to your total scores for that lesson? Why or why not?

Go down to Graph 2 and shade your scores for the lesson you just completed.

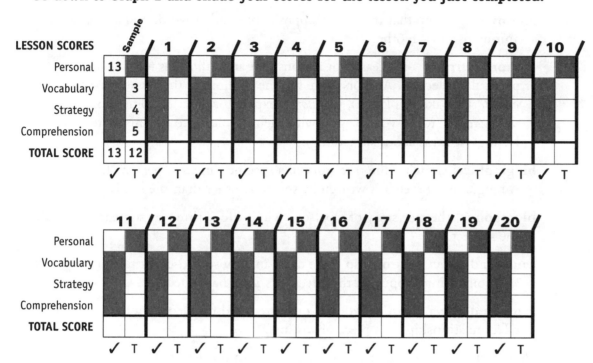

Graph 2

Now record your overall progress. In the first column for the lesson you just completed, shade the number of squares that match your Personal Checklist score. In the second column for that lesson, shade the number of squares that match your total score. As you fill in this graph, you will be able to check your progress across the book.

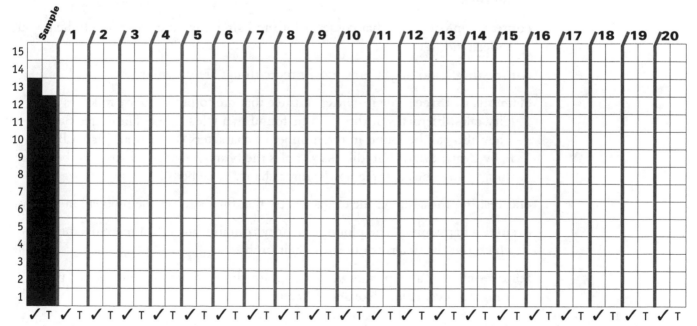

Glossary of Terms

This glossary includes definitions for important terms introduced in this book.

antonym   a word that means the opposite of another word. *Fast* and *slow* are antonyms of each other.

author's purpose   the reason or reasons that an author has for writing a particular selection. Authors write for one or more of these purposes: to *entertain* (make you laugh), to *inform* (explain or describe something), to *persuade* (try to get you to agree with their opinion), to *express* (share their feelings or ideas about something).

biographical sketch   the true story of a specific time in a person's life. A biographical sketch is written by someone other than the subject.

biography   the true story of a person's whole life, written by someone other than the subject.

cause-and-effect relationship   the cause in a cause-and-effect relationship tells *why* something happened; the effect tells *what* happened.

cause-and-effect chain   a graphic organizer used for recording the cause-and-effect relationships in a piece of writing.

characters   the people or animals that perform the action in a story.

comparing   looking at how two or more things are alike.

compound word   a word that is made up of two words put together. *Handlebars* and *weekend* are examples of compound words.

concept map   a graphic organizer used for recording the main ideas and supporting details in a piece of writing.

conclusion   a decision that is reached after thinking about certain facts or information.

context   information that comes before and after a word or situation to help you understand it.

contrasting   looking at how two or more things are different.

elements of three   the instances of three that are found in many folktales and fairy tales. Elements of three can be found in a tale's title ("The Three Bears"). They also can be found in the number of characters (Papa Bear, Mama Bear, Baby Bear); events (Goldilocks samples the bears' porridge, chairs, and beds); or things (three bears, three bowls, three chairs, three beds).

end result   the solution the characters try that finally solves the problem in a story.

event   a happening. The plot of any story contains one or more events during which the characters try to solve their problems.

features chart   a graphic organizer used for showing how several people, places, things, or events are alike and different.

fairy tale   a story with at least one of the following elements: imaginary characters, imaginary objects, an imaginary setting, imaginary events, and elements of three.

fiction   stories about made-up characters or events. Forms of fiction include short stories, historical fiction, fairy tales, folktales, and myths.

folktale   a story whose characters are often animals that act like people. Their personalities are usually "flat," or one-sided. For example, a character might be clever and hard-working or foolish and lazy.

graphic organizer   a chart, graph, or drawing used to show how the main ideas in a piece of writing are organized and related.

headings   the short titles given throughout a piece of nonfiction. The headings often state the main ideas of a selection.

historical fiction   a made-up story based on real historical facts or events.

informational article   a piece of writing that gives facts and details about a particular subject, or topic.

main idea   the most important idea of a paragraph, section, or whole piece of writing.

main idea table   a graphic organizer used for recording the main ideas and supporting details in a piece of writing.

main idea sentence   the sentence that tells what a paragraph, section, or whole piece of writing is about. The rest of the paragraph, section, or piece contains supporting details that tell more about the main idea.

multiple-meaning word   a word that has more than one meaning. The word *beat* is a multiple-meaning word whose meanings include "defeat," "mark time in music," and "mix with a spoon."

myth   a story that usually explains something in nature, such as why there are solar eclipses or why elephants have trunks.

nonfiction   writing that gives facts and information about real people, events, and topics. Informational articles, biographical sketches, and biographies are some forms of nonfiction.

outline   a framework for organizing the most important ideas in a piece of writing. Some outlines are organized according to a system of Roman numerals (I, II, III, IV, V, and so on) and capital letters (A, B, C, D, E, and so on).

plot   the sequence of events in a piece of writing.

prediction   a kind of guess that is made based on the context clues given in a story.

problem   difficulty or question that a character must solve or answer.

problem-solution frame   a graphic organizer used for recording the problem, solutions, and end result in a piece of writing.

sequence   the order of events in a piece of writing. The sequence shows what happens or what to do first, second, and so on.

sequence chain   a graphic organizer used for recording the sequence of events in a piece of writing. Sequence chains are used mostly for shorter selections or periods of time, and time lines are used mostly for longer selections or periods of time.

setting   the time and place in which a story happens.

signal words   words and phrases that tell when something happens or when to do something. Examples of signal words are *first, next, then, finally, after lunch,* and *two years later.*

solution   the things that characters or people do to solve a problem.

specialized vocabulary   words that are related to a particular subject, or topic. Specialized vocabulary words in "Laughter Is Good Medicine" include *cure, disease, germs, immune system,* and *blood pressure.*

story map   a graphic organizer used for recording the main parts of a story: its title, setting, character, problem, events, and solution.

suffix   a word part that is added to the end of a word. Adding a suffix usually changes the word's meaning and function. For example, the suffix *-less* means "without," so the word *painless* changes from the noun *pain* to an adjective meaning "without pain."

summary   a short description. A summary describes what has happened in a piece of fiction, or what the main ideas are in a piece of nonfiction.

supporting details   details that describe or explain the main idea of a paragraph, section, or whole piece of text.

synonym   a word that has the same meaning as another word. *Fast* and *quick* are synonyms of each other.

time line   a graphic organizer used for recording the sequence of events in a piece of writing. Time lines are used mostly for longer selections or periods of time, and sequence chains are used mostly for shorter selections or periods of time.

topic   the subject of a piece of writing. The topic is what the selection is all about.

traditional tale   a story that was originally passed on by word of mouth. Traditional tales usually try to explain why people behave in certain ways or why things happen in nature. Traditional tales include fairy tales, folktales, and myths.

Venn diagram   a graphic organizer used for showing how two people, places, things, or events are alike and different.

Acknowledgments

Acknowledgment is gratefully made to the following publishers, authors, and agents for permission to reprint these works. Every effort has been made to determine copyright owners. In the case of any omissions, the Publisher will be pleased to make suitable acknowledgments in future editions.

"All Kinds of Money" from *Money* by Robert Young. Copyright 1998 by Carolrhoda Books, Inc. Used by permission of the publisher. All Rights Reserved.

From *The Drinking Gourd* by F. N. Monjo. Text copyright © 1970 by F. N. Monjo. Used by permission of HarperCollins Publishers.

The Fisherman Who Needed a Knife by Marie Winn. Reprinted by permission of the author.

From *Flash, Crash, Rumble, and Roll* by Franklyn M. Branley. Used by permission of HarperCollins Publishers.

"Grandaddy's Place" from *Grandaddy's Place* by Helen V. Griffith. Copyright © 1987 by Helen V. Griffith. By Permission of Greenwillow Books, a division of William Morrow and Company, Inc.

"Greg LeMond" from *Comeback! Four True Stories* by Jim O'Connor. Copyright © 1992 by Jim O'Connor. Reprinted by permission of Random House, Inc.

"Harriet Tubman" from *Harriet Tubman* by Margo McLoone. Reprinted by permission of Capstone Press Inc.

"The Hole in the Road" by Helen Ketteman. Copyright © 1997 by Helen Ketteman. First appeared in *Spider Magazine*. Published by The Cricket Magazine Group. Reprinted by permission of Curtis Brown, Ltd.

"On Bicycles" from *On Bicycles* by Kyle Carter. Copyright © 1994. The Rourke Press, Inc. Permission granted by Rourke Press.

"Ostriches or The Birds Nobody Noticed" by Angela Mackworth-Young, writer and storyteller, from an ever-expanding collection of stories called *The Zushkaali Stories*. Reprinted by permission of the author.

"Petronella" from *The Practical Princess and Other Liberating Fairy Tales* by Jay Williams. Published by Parents' Magazine Press. Copyright © 1978 by Jay Williams. Reprinted by permission of Scholastic, Inc.

"The Pudding Like a Night on the Sea" from *The Stories Julian Tells* by Ann Cameron, illustrated by Ann Strugnell. Text copyright © 1981 by Ann Cameron. Illustrations Copyright © 1981 by Ann Strugnell. Reprinted by permission of Pantheon Books, a division of Random House, Inc.

"The Stars: Lights in the Night Sky" from *The Stars: Lights in the Night Sky* by Jeanne Bendick. Text © 1991 Jeanne Bendick. Illustrations © 1991 Eagle Books Limited. Brookfield, CT: The Millbrook Press Inc.